Providing Reference Services

PRACTICAL GUIDES FOR LIBRARIANS

◎ About the Series

This innovative series written and edited for librarians by librarians provides authoritative, practical information and guidance on a wide spectrum of library processes and operations.

Books in the series are focused, describing practical and innovative solutions to a problem facing today's librarian and delivering step-by-step guidance for planning, creating, implementing, managing, and evaluating a wide range of services and programs.

The books are aimed at beginning and intermediate librarians needing basic instruction/guidance in a specific subject and at experienced librarians who need to gain knowledge in a new area or guidance in implementing a new program/service.

◎ About the Series Editor

The **Practical Guides for Librarians** series was conceived by and is edited by M. Sandra Wood, MLS, MBA, AHIP, FMLA, Librarian Emerita, Penn State University Libraries.

M. Sandra Wood was a librarian at the George T. Harrell Library, the Milton S. Hershey Medical Center, College of Medicine, Pennsylvania State University, Hershey, PA, for over thirty-five years, specializing in reference, educational, and database services. Ms. Wood worked for several years as a development editor for Neal-Schuman Publishers.

Ms. Wood received an MLS from Indiana University and an MBA from the University of Maryland. She is a fellow of the Medical Library Association and served as a member of MLA's Board of Directors from 1991 to 1995. Ms. Wood is founding and current editor of *Medical Reference Services Quarterly*, now in its thirty-fifth volume. She also was founding editor of the *Journal of Consumer Health on the Internet* and the *Journal of Electronic Resources in Medical Libraries* and served as editor/coeditor of both journals through 2011.

Titles in the Series

1. *How to Teach: A Practical Guide for Librarians* by Beverley E. Crane.
2. *Implementing an Inclusive Staffing Model for Today's Reference Services* by Julia K. Nims, Paula Storm, and Robert Stevens.
3. *Managing Digital Audiovisual Resources: A Practical Guide for Librarians* by Matthew C. Mariner.
4. *Outsourcing Technology: A Practical Guide for Librarians* by Robin Hastings

Providing Reference Services

A Practical Guide for Librarians

John Gottfried
Katherine Pennavaria

PRACTICAL GUIDES FOR LIBRARIANS, NO. 32

ROWMAN & LITTLEFIELD
Lanham • Boulder • New York • London

Published by Rowman & Littlefield
A wholly owned subsidiary of The Rowman & Littlefield Publishing Group, Inc.
4501 Forbes Boulevard, Suite 200, Lanham, Maryland 20706
www.rowman.com

Unit A, Whitacre Mews, 26-34 Stannary Street, London SE11 4AB

British Library Cataloguing in Publication Information Available

Library of Congress Cataloging-in-Publication Data

Names: Gottfried, John, 1953– author. | Pennavaria, Katherine, 1959– author.
Title: Providing reference services : a practical guide for librarians / John Gottfried, Katherine
Pennavaria.
Description: Lanham : Rowman & Littlefield, [2017] | Series: Practical guides for librarians ; 32
| Includes bibliographical references and index.
Identifiers: LCCN 2017001823 (print) | LCCN 2017021316 (ebook) | ISBN 9781442279124
(electronic) | ISBN 9781442279117 (pbk. : alk. paper)
Subjects: LCSH: Reference services (Libraries) | Reference services (Libraries)—United States.
Classification: LCC Z711 (ebook) | LCC Z711 .G68 2017 (print) | DDC 025.5/2—dc23
LC record available at https://lccn.loc.gov/2017001823

Printed in the United States of America

To my wife, Linda Gottfried.—John Gottfried

To my partner, Donna McKay Kasznel.—Katherine Pennavaria

Contents

Figures and Tables

⊚ Figures

⊚ Tables

Preface

Some might suggest that this book shouldn't exist at all. Many library critics, after all—and even a few librarians—believe that reference services are archaic endeavors, like making buggy whips or operating a telephone switchboard. Not that these are bad professions, the thinking goes—they are simply no longer very useful. On the way to obsolescence, however, a funny thing has happened to library reference services. While changed in nature and exhibiting very different patterns of usage, reference services have nonetheless survived, and, in some institutions, thrived. Why is this so?

Providing Reference Services: A Practical Guide for Librarians examines the relevance of reference services to today's libraries and their patrons. Chapters will dissect and inspect library reference from many perspectives: history, evolution, current practices, and even the amorphous future. The authors draw on extensive research, endless questions to colleagues, and the lessons of personal experience, all gathered in the hope that distilling reference services down to their essence will yield at least a few useful truths. At the end of our journey, though, we may have no better explanation for the continued resilience of reference services than this: libraries have always been a large and wondrous—sometimes even intimidating—source of knowledge. While librarians labor to make resources easy to find and use, locating what you need in a library can still be challenging. It is true that digital access to information has made some types of information easier to find, but it has made sorting this information into coherent blocks of useful knowledge more complicated. Monographs, articles, theses, dissertations, documents, videos, tweets, blogs, forums, and chats all contribute to the sum of our collective wisdom and know-how, and all must be accessible to the modern researcher in manageable form.

Who can help with such a task? Google and Bing and their search-engine brethren? The unforgiving algorithms of Google can find the tip of the iceberg of knowledge, but the parts below the surface are often the best. You will not find the help you need through Amazon.com or from the "Blue Shirts" at Best Buy. The best computers and mobile devices in the world are mere tools, and not nearly as smart as they purport to be, Apple spokes-entity Siri notwithstanding. For researchers and readers lost in the maze of the information age, the best hope for effective assistance and support is still, as it has been for many years, the reference librarian. Reference librarians provide guidance supported by training and experience, almost always delivered with a smile, and offered free of charge or very close to it. A helping human hand may have seemed outmoded even a few years back, but the human touch does seem to be regaining its value across our cold, digital world.

Purpose

This book was created to be a useful field manual for reference services practitioners trying to maintain the honorable library tradition of guiding researchers through their darkest hours. The objective was to gather the most useful advice to help reference services supervisors and librarians gain confidence and competence in the practice of their craft. On the rare instances when the authors venture into academic theory or abstract controversies, it is solely to provide deeper comprehension of a practical point. Experienced reference librarians and library novices alike should find much that is helpful in this work. Wherever possible, the materials in this book were developed to be useful for librarians in any type of library that might provide reference services, including academic, public, school, and other specialized libraries.

Recurring Themes

Several basic themes run through this work, appearing and reappearing, and reiterating points that, while obvious to many, bear repeating through the sheer weight of their fundamental importance.

- *The mission, vision, and values of the organization should reflect themselves in every level of activity in a library.* Whether these relate to the lofty academic ideals of a major research university, the simple desire to educate and entertain at the local public library, or the profit objectives of a corporate library, the horses must all pull the cart in the same direction, or it will never reach the market. However small your part in this big picture, you should strive to make your efforts count toward organizational goals.
- *Librarians must know their clientele.* Providing excellent reference services requires knowing who your patrons are, the kinds of problems they face, and the types of library services and materials will be most helpful to them.
- *Librarians must be the solution to their patrons' problems.* You must prove yourself useful to your patrons by solving their problems. Ideally, you seek to be the best solution, the easiest to access, and the most cost effective.
- *Librarians must document their accomplishments.* In the current fiscal environment, every library (and every librarian) should be prepared to defend their funding, their methods, and even their existence to those who control the finances. Remember that the kinds of people who control finances are most often the kinds of people who respect quantifiable evidence, where value is expressed in the most objective terms possible.

Organization of the Book

This book is arranged to provide an orderly journey through the vast and varied world of reference services. It starts with general topics, then moves to more specific areas requiring more specialized knowledge and methods. As far as possible, each chapter is a freestanding element of the whole, which can be read and implemented in isolation from the other chapters. As noted above, however, there are themes and approaches that cross over and interplay among the different chapters, so the best approach is at least a cursory reading from beginning to end, returning to relevant sections of the book as needed.

Chapter 1 covers the fundamentals of the field. Basic terms are defined, and the rich history of reference services is reviewed in some detail. There is a discussion of more recent advancements, with an examination of the relationship between research instruction and reference services.

Chapter 2 focuses on the sources used for reference services. While this book is not designed to provide in-depth coverage of reference sources, a general overview of sources will provide some understanding of the kinds of materials reference librarians use to help their patrons. This chapter also discusses development of the reference collection in both paper and electronic formats, along with consideration of the concept of "ready reference" (the small collection of reference sources kept near the reference desk or other point of contact for reference).

Chapter 3 deals with some of the nuts and bolts of providing reference services. The nature and quality of the interaction between reference librarian and patron is covered, along with a review of virtual reference (reference carried out through various technologies) and other emerging trends.

Chapter 4 looks at issues related to the people who perform reference services. Practical methods and approaches to staff planning are discussed, along with advice on the process of recruiting and selecting effective reference staff. There are also useful guidelines for common human resources practices such as training, supervising, and performing staff evaluations.

Chapter 5 provides insight on the difficult tasks related to reference services administration. This includes comments on the precarious nature of middle management for reference services, as well a call to make the connection between reference services goals and those of the library as a whole. The challenging and (for many librarians) distasteful task of responding to library budgets and financial documents is covered, along with the increasing emphasis on carrying out thorough assessments of library services.

Chapter 6 covers a variety of perspectives and techniques for marketing library reference services. The chapter begins with a broad discussion of the nature of library outreach. Library marketing is then defined, with an introduction to identifying the market for your library services, and tips for breaking that market down into distinct segments. The general steps involved in developing and delivering a marketing plan are presented. There is also a section discussing practical considerations for collaborations between reference services and potential partners both inside and outside of the library.

Chapter 7 gazes into the future of reference services, and examines several issues that may impact the way reference services are managed and delivered in the coming years. The existence of current and potential competitors for the library's role as a provider of reference services is discussed, along with the need to deal effectively with new innovations and technologies. Specific technologies and services likely to emerge and grow in importance are reviewed as well.

Making Best Use of *Providing Reference Services: A Practical Guide for Librarians*

Mentioned previously were several themes that appear and reappear throughout this book, but to this list one more must be added—remember as you read that every topic discussed and every point made are merely the beginning of a long, interactive conversation, rather than the last word. The authors are themselves practitioners in the trenches of reference services and would never presume to identify a single answer for any question. There is always another perspective, a contrary opinion and, if there is not, there certainly should be. As Erica Jong once noted, there is no such thing as a still life. By the time this book appears in your hand, things will have changed, if subtly; reference services will have shifted and become something new again.

If this is the beginning of your journey in library reference services, welcome and hold on to your hat—it's going to be a bumpy ride, but it will also be a fascinating and ultimately rewarding one. If you are a weary fellow traveler long out on the reference services trail, feel free to pick through the contents of this chapters, taking what you need and discarding the rest. All are welcome—your hard work and unique voice will be needed to maintain the vitality and relevance of library reference services through many challenges in the years to come.

Acknowledgments

We gratefully acknowledge the support and encouragement of our Western Kentucky University Library colleagues, especially Brian Coutts, head of the Library Public Services Department; Connie Foster, dean of University Libraries; Rosemary Meszaros, coordinator of Government Documents and Law; and research assistant Jessica Barksdale. We also appreciate the guidance and hard work of our editor, M. Sandra Wood of Rowman & Littlefield.

CHAPTER 1

What Are Library Reference Services?

IN THIS CHAPTER

▷ Defining "reference services"

▷ Exploring the early history of reference

▷ Following reference developments into the modern age, and establishing research instruction as an important part of reference service

---

REFERENCE SERVICES HAVE BEEN AROUND for as long as people in libraries and archives have been answering questions. And libraries have been around since start of the human written record, around 2600 BCE. Long before the texts known as the Hebrew Bible or the Old Testament came to be created, the ancient Sumerians created and preserved clay tablets with cuneiform writing on them, and these were usually kept together in what can only be called an archive or library. Historians consider these collections of written records to be the end of prehistory and the beginning of history (Renfrew, 2008). It was the ancient Greeks, though, who created the template for the private library in Western civilization, and that model eventually led to the establishment of library collections owned by institutions, which is the norm for most libraries today.

So in general terms, humans have collected, preserved, stored, and organized information in written form for about 5,000 years. But long before that, communities of humans found ways to preserve local and family knowledge, usually by establishing an oral tradition of storytelling and fact-repeating that was passed down through generations. And those oral traditions have lasted well beyond the development of written history. The famous epic poem Beowulf, from about 900 CE, or the Anglo-Saxon period of English history, is thought by many scholars to have originated as an oral composition performed by a bard or singer called a *scop*. A *scop* was primarily an itinerant storyteller who performed in exchange for money or barter; his storytelling was valued for entertainment, but also for keeping Anglo-Saxon history, cultural details, and social conventions alive through the stories.

Quite often, storytellers became the musicians of their cultures, keeping tribal and community history alive through recitation set to music. Even today, such traditions still exist—in the Balkan region, for example, singers known as *guslari* still perform on a stringed instrument (*gusle*) while singing long narrative tales about local history (www .britannica.com/art/guslar). In West Africa, the person who functions as historian, storyteller, poet, and musician for a community is called a *griot*.

In addition to reciting or singing the histories they memorized or the stories they created, throughout history these knowledge keepers were undoubtedly called on to answer questions from time to time. They can be considered the first providers of reference services.

⑨ Defining Reference Services

The last official definition for reference services was approved by the Reference and User Services Association (RUSA), which is part of the American Library Association, in 2008. RUSA distinguishes between reference *transactions* and reference *work*. A reference transaction is an "information consultation" during which someone on the library staff works with another person to help that person meet a "particular information need." During a reference transaction, the staff member uses information sources in a variety of ways, including interpreting, evaluating, and recommending them on behalf of the patron (http://www.ala.org/rusa/resources/guidelines/definitionsreference). Excluded from reference transactions are formal research instruction sessions, which would be counted under another heading.

Reference *work*, on the other hand, means reference transactions that involve creating, managing, and/or assessing information tools and resources. Therefore, a library staff member who compiles a help sheet for students in a particular class is doing reference work; helping an individual student with the work in that class, however, is a reference transaction. The creation of research guides and specialized web pages counts here as well. By this definition, much of what library staff members do falls under the category of reference work. In fact, everyone who works in any public-service capacity in a library can be said to do reference work as a significant part of the job.

In formal statistics keeping, some of the questions fielded by staff do not count as specifically reference questions—the Association of Research Libraries (ARL) and National Center for Education Statistics (NCES) both make a distinction between questions like "Where is the bathroom?" and requests for assistance finding information on Civil War generals (www.arlstatistics.org and https://nces.ed.gov/surveys/libraries/). But in general, answering questions is what reference services providers do. They also recommend further avenues of research, comment on the quality of sources, and suggest refinements to a topic.

Essentially, the role of reference services providers is multifaceted. In addition to answering questions, these providers also teach users how to find information for themselves and how to use library resources. The primacy of the research instruction role over the question-answering and book-advisory role was slow to develop, but most reference services administrators today recognize that professional-level assistance involves instruction, toward the reasonable goal of helping users become independent of the librarian.

In early 2016, RUSA president Anne M. Houston addressed the issue of how to define reference services for our time. She says that while the last formal definition was made in 2008, the organization has never stopped reviewing and considering all aspects of reference. In "What's in a Name? Toward a New Definition of Reference," Houston addresses RUSA members: "Do you refer to yourself as a reference librarian?" (186). She notes that the methods and practices of reference services have changed much over time, but the same phrase is still used. Does the term still accurately describe the "scope and focus" of RUSA? If not, what better terminology might be considered? A 2014 survey of RUSA members yielded no clear answer: just under half of the respondents rejected a name change. About 50 percent of the remaining half (about 25 percent of all respondents) voted to change the name, and the other 25 percent either didn't have an opinion or didn't answer the question.

Regardless of whether RUSA decides to change its name, Houston's larger point is important: reference services have evolved so much that a new definition is necessary. Since 2008, when the last official definition was created, social media has become a go-to source for information. Access to resources using mobile devices, in its infancy in 2008, has become the norm. Houston (2016) says that to meet the needs of library users in today's environment, the concept of reference services must be redefined to include these skills that contemporary librarians use, but have not been traditionally part of reference work training:

- *Consulting/advising.* Helping users with "complex tasks that require managing, formatting, storing, using, or displaying information" (e.g., demonstrating a citation management tool, recommending a slide-sharing app, explaining copyright laws and limitations) (187).
- *Teaching.* Users need "life skills related to technology and information management" (187), which reference providers are in a unique position to offer. Teaching in this context can take place in a classroom, in a workshop, at the reference desk, or even in the stacks.
- *Interpreting.* The work of reference providers requires above-average communication ability. Such workers also need to know "how our systems are specific to a unique Western-based library culture and how that culture may be difficult for a user to understand" (188). Libraries are full of non-native English speakers; reference providers must interpret the library for them, and also "translate" its norms and conventions.
- *Advocating.* Public services librarians and staff know that they serve as advocates for their library. In fact, the most successful reference transactions include an element of advocacy. Daily interactions can "build a positive image and rapport with users" (188), and librarians can also advocate on behalf of patrons by requesting products and contributing to improvement in systems design.
- *Programming.* Effective programs are vital for a library's connection to its community. Librarian-style programming involves not computer code, but planning "workshops, book talks, lectures, displays, and exhibits" (188). Training in reference librarianship needs to include the skills required to program events, plan the effective use of space, and contribute to the graphic design of signage, displays, and web pages.
- *User experience.* Public services librarians are "front-line staff" (188), and thus in position to observe where user-experience design succeeds or fails. Reference providers must work with user-experience specialists to design systems that work for targeted patron groups.

- *Design thinking.* Rather than repeating successful designs and programs from the past, why not "reboot with more flexible options that dynamically evolve on the basis of user feedback?" (188). The skill of design thinking involves pondering each new step and considering whether the past is an adequate guide to the way forward. Perhaps most libraries need fixed shelving, but maybe yours does not, given the unique needs of its patrons.

What's important about Houston's list is that she arrived at it by closely examining the questions asked and help given in many complex reference transactions. Generations ago, questioners sought factual answers to fairly simple questions, which usually started with an interrogative word that established the need for a simple fact (What? Who? When? Where?). Today, however, the leading word is usually "How?": How can I check out e-books? How do I find my class in Blackboard? How do I convert EBSCO citations to MLA? How do I access JSTOR remotely? Houston also studied carefully the actual daily activities of public services librarians: the displays created, the workshops planned, the web pages maintained.

A History of Reference

Until recently, the best resource for anyone seeking information to answer simple questions was a printed book. Most libraries today are still stocked with thick reference volumes that contain densely detailed information traditionally available nowhere else (for more about reference collections, see chapter 2). But the Internet changed that centuries-old paradigm, and today's reference books often sit unused on the shelves. Reference providers have long recognized that educating library users on the *quality* of reference sources is an important part of their job. It's not enough just to answer questions; it's important to show why this answer, or this approach to obtaining the answer, is superior to another one.

Let's go back in time for a bit. Until the twentieth century, libraries played one primary role: they housed and preserved printed materials. Librarians, it follows, were charged primarily with doing the purchasing, processing, and protecting of said materials. But for much of written history, those materials did not "circulate"—patrons could not go to the collection storehouse and walk out with books. Until circulating libraries were developed in the eighteenth century, libraries were places a person visited to consult the collection, take notes, and then leave (and not everyone was allowed access to the collection). The first circulating, or subscription, libraries were for-profit ventures, designed to make recently published books available to subscribers at a cost lower than purchasing each volume individually (much like Netflix, today's most successful streaming and disc service). Over time, the profit angle disappeared as tax-supported public libraries became the norm. And as public libraries solidified their place in communities, the role of the librarian grew well beyond that of simply collecting, cataloging, and protecting books.

Reference in the Late Nineteenth Century

University libraries have been around since the Middle Ages; use was generally restricted to students and other members of the academic institution. These libraries did not pioneer the notion of reference services. No, that happened in public libraries, which started appearing around the middle of the nineteenth century. As public libraries increasingly appeared in cities and rural communities, they not only replaced subscription libraries, but also prompted an evolving role for librarians.

A major change to the librarian's role started the same year the American Library Association (ALA) came into being, and the year Alexander Graham Bell obtained a patent for the telephone. In 1876, Samuel Swett Green, a librarian and founding member of ALA, published an article that encouraged librarians to see their role in broader terms. Published in the second issue of *Library Journal*, Green's article, "Personal Relations Between Librarians and Readers," is generally seen as the first professional publication to address reference services in libraries. His title hints at the then-prevalent assumption that users of libraries were primarily *readers*, and that people came to libraries to read. Green was in no doubt, however, that people who came into libraries did so because they needed something: "Persons who use a popular library for purposes of investigation generally need a great deal of assistance" (1876: S4). What he meant was that most people coming in were unsure how the library worked, or whether they were even allowed to ask questions. And he was correct—for most members of the public in 1876, the chance to go into a library and get assistance was a relatively new phenomenon. Green had greater confidence in the ability of "scholars and persons of high social position" (S4) to state their information needs clearly and without hesitation (a questionable assumption), but said that these individuals also needed some guidance.

Green suggested, in a more meandering than targeted way, that the modern public librarian should fulfill four essential functions:

- guide users in the use of the library
- assist users in finding answers to inquiries
- advise users in selecting quality reading material
- promote the library to users and to the local community

What he describes, in other words, is a more specialized role: the *public-services* (or *information-services*) librarian's duties (reference services, community outreach, research assistance) as separate from the duties of the *technical services* librarian (ordering, cataloging, securing).

Today Green's approach to library users, at least the non-scholarly ones, might be called "proactive." If someone asks a question, he says, don't let that person leave until the information need is satisfied! Rather, think of the library user the way a shopkeeper thinks of customers; if necessary: "hold on to them until they have obtained the information they are seeking" (1876: S5). He also recommends helping users become less dependent on the librarian by teaching them how to do research—something necessary at that time, because public libraries were drawing in large numbers of people who had little idea of how libraries worked.

With Green's article, and the launching of the ALA, the public services librarian's role was set out in terms that have not changed all that much even today. However, Green wrote at a time when the ability to answer questions and look up information depended solely on the books and other writings present in the librarian's space. As noted above, Bell's patent for the telephone was granted in 1876, but the availability of phones in libraries was still a long way off. Green, in his role as librarian at the Worcester, Massachusetts, Free Public Library, could not consult a knowledgeable colleague who lived at a distance unless he sent a letter or telegram. So, it fell to librarians to be repositories of knowledge about the collections they oversaw, and to answer information queries with the resources at hand.

After Green's article appeared and the ALA was launched, librarianship was forever altered. The remainder of the nineteenth century brought significant changes in both public and academic libraries, and librarians began reinventing their jobs. Catalogs expanded and became more flexible, moving from printed lists to the more familiar card version. Classification schemes were developed that allowed similar titles to be grouped together, as an aid to serendipity while shelf browsing. According to Louis Kaplan (1964), by 1893 one-third of the 200 largest U.S. colleges had full-time librarians; they replaced professors who had been volunteering part time to fulfill librarian responsibilities. In both public and academic libraries, reference-specific book collections were separated out from the main circulating collection, and in most libraries, rooms or areas devoted to reference services were established.

By the way, the term *librarian* has not always been used to mean what it means today (a professional with a degree in library or information science), so it's impossible to know, when reading some of the earliest literature on the role of librarians, what exactly was meant by the term. The director or head of a library almost certainly had some training, but what about the people who provided reference services? Most likely, the term *librarian* was used then to mean anyone who worked or provided services in a library (the same mistake happens occasionally today).

One of the first publications that directly addressed the evolving role public libraries played within a community appeared in 1894. In *Public Libraries in America*, William Isaac Fletcher, a librarian at Amherst College, stated unequivocally: "Every public library should be a library of reference . . . the supplying of books for home-reading must not be regarded as the only function of the library" (1894: 73). Academic libraries have always played that role, he points out, and too often the public library has been considered the lighter option—a place mainly to check out books and get suggestions for reading. Fletcher wanted that to change.

Today's large communities usually have a library system with multiple branches or locations. The staff members in these separate locations usually work together to serve their patrons' needs, and when someone at any public library branch needs specialized help with a reference inquiry, they often turn to their compatriots in a nearby academic library. Unconnected libraries also share printed books and electronic copies of articles among themselves via interlibrary loan. But that paradigm was not always the operative one; someone had to articulate a vision for such sharing and cooperation. In the last few years of the nineteenth century, that someone stepped up. His name was Charles Davidson, of the University of the State of New York, which is not a school but an accreditation body that still today establishes the standards for New York state educational institutions. Davidson gave a talk at the 1898 ALA conference (published in *Library Journal* later that same year) that laid out his vision for reference services, not just within, but between and among libraries. His impassioned words are worth quoting in full:

> There should be such connection between our large libraries and the small ones that the investigator in a small town may turn to his librarian, have his question passed on, and receive from the large library the full bibliography bearing upon his subject. To this should be added also an exchange of books far broader and more liberal than obtains at present . . . it is not true that the same student working in a little library in a small town can command all works in any library in the country. This should be possible and practicable (1898: 141).

Possible and practicable, yes, but still just a vision in 1898. Today the patrons of small libraries do, in fact, have access to much larger collections and information sources. The "access versus ownership" debate is over—access matters more. But in Davidson's day, a library user's access to information and to printed reading material was only as good as his or her location. Citizens in large urban areas could count on greater access because their libraries were bigger. People in small towns just weren't so lucky. But things were about to change.

Reference in the Early Twentieth Century

Even though cooperation among libraries was still a thing of the future when the new century ticked over, the role of librarian as provider of reference services was well established by the time the photograph in figure 1.1 was taken.

The photograph shows a long, curved, wooden desk at the Library of Congress Reading Room, behind which stands a group of formally dressed library employees. This image clearly indicates the austerity and seriousness that greeted a library user approaching that desk. Note also the thick tomes piled somewhat precariously in front of the men; perhaps they had recently been used to answer a reference inquiry.

The superintendent of that very reading room, Walter Warner Bishop, addressed the subject of reference services in his 1915 article published in the *Bulletin of the American Library Association*. He defined what he called "reference work" as "help given to a reader" in pursuit of a research task (1). He also referred to any employee assigned the task of assisting library users ("readers") as "reference librarians," and said that those individuals

Figure 1.1.　The Library of Congress Main Reading Room, c. 1911 (left to right: Charles Wallace Collins, Ernest Kletsch, Maurice Hussey Avery, and Hugh A. Morrison). http://www.loc.gov/loc/lcib/02034/digital-ref.html. *Source:* Library of Congress, Manuscript Division, LC Archives, PIO series, #599

were "the interpreters of the library to the public" (1). Bishop didn't add much to the evolving discussion of what, exactly, reference work consisted of, but his is one of the earliest articles to contain the phrase "reference" in the title.

It should be noted that the rate of change was faster for public librarians than for academic ones, who held on longer to the "custodian of the books" paradigm that had for so long defined their role. But certainly by the first years of the twentieth century, reference services as a separate function had become part of most public and academic libraries. As the demand for answers to complex questions and for assistance with complex research projects grew, college and university librarians began to specialize, to become expert bibliographers and reference providers in more narrowly defined subject areas. Around this time, "special" library collections and reference services also began to develop within institutions not necessarily associated with libraries, such as law offices, corporations, and hospitals. The focus of the librarian in those special collections, for the most part, was usually on answering questions, and not so much on instructing users in research methods or advising them on quality reading material.

Over the first few decades of the twentieth century, Bell Telephone totally transformed communication throughout the world, and libraries were as much affected as every other institution. In 1927, the first trans-Atlantic connection was established. By 1928, there were millions of telephones in service across the nation's cities, each of them a potential source of inquiry directed to reference staff. A mere 50 years after Samuel Green penned his gentle plea for librarians to expand their role, librarians were dealing with inquiries Green could never have imagined. Green was accustomed to dealing with patrons face to face; his public library, by its very nature of being a building in a specific place, was not likely to be visited by large numbers of people on any given day.

As occurred earlier in the developing history of reference services, public and academic libraries were affected differently. As public library reference staff experienced a sharp rise in the number of inquiries fielded because of the new telephone technology, they began to refer more complicated, research-oriented inquiries to the nearest university librarians. In other words, public library staff were able to handle the vastly increased quantity only by sorting by quality: questions that could be easily answered by a quick consultation of a printed book they would handle; everything else was passed along to the specialists. But university libraries were about to undergo their own surge in quantity as World War II ended and military personnel by the thousands took advantage of the 1944 GI Bill and enrolled in college and university classes. The need for professional quality reference services for large numbers of students forced university libraries to change into something like we know today.

In 1930, one of the first research-based textbooks aimed at students of library science was issued. In that book, *Reference Work: A Textbook for Students of Library Work and Librarians*, James I. Wyer discussed the nature and advisability of reference assistance for several types of work that students normally did in university and college libraries. The students' use of the library, he said, falls into these categories:

- *Prescribed reading*. Student comes to the library to read something assigned for class.
- *Required but not prescribed work*. Student comes to the library to write an assigned essay or research paper.
- *Voluntary library use*. Student comes to the library to seek information or materials unconnected with classwork.

In each case, Wyer recommended minimal interaction on the part of the reference librarian: "A word here, a question there, a suggestion now and then" (192). Otherwise, he says, leave the student "to find himself among books, catalogs, and indexes." His strange, almost counterintuitive advice seems to have come from his interviews with university library staff, who apparently told him that they didn't really get all that many questions from students, and that the questions they did get were "almost wholly in regard to courses and reserves" (192). As Roseanne M. Cordell puts it rather tartly, there might be any number of reasons why students would hesitate to ask questions in a college library, "but that students didn't need assistance with research is probably not one of [them]" (2013: 3).

A year later, in 1931, Dr. Shiyali Ramamrita Ranganathan, a mathematician and librarian from India, published his famous "Five Laws of Library Science." The list, as given in Kabir (2003: 454), has a curious mixture of elliptical sentences that are anything but parallel:

- Books are for use.
- Every book its reader.
- Every reader his book.
- Save the time of the reader.
- A library is a growing organism.

Though his list has been reinterpreted and modified many times since 1931, we note with interest that in its original form, Ranganathan's list contains not a word about providing reference services. His list applies to "library science," but the work of assisting library users with personal, professional, or scholarly inquiries plays no part in the scheme. Clearly, reference services, especially in academic libraries, still had a long way to go.

By the mid-1930s, telephone reference was well established in urban public libraries. In a 1936 article published in *Library Journal*, Emily Garnett suggested a detailed plan for providing reference services. She covered the logistical and staffing basics, suggested which printed materials needed to be kept close at hand ("ready reference"), and discussed the various types of questions that might be encountered. The most interesting thing about Garnett's article, however, is the distinction she made regarding the social status of the people who might call in. "Club women," she said, "should not be encouraged to expect too much of this service" (909). The reason? Those women, almost all technically unemployed, weren't usually calling to get "an answer to definite questions." Also, "they are women who have the time to make a leisurely search at the library" (909). Businessmen and other professionals, on the other hand, were entitled to A-1 service: "They usually want concise information which is needed immediately, and they have less time to come to the library" (910). While we can applaud this early focus on providing dedicated reference work, the suggestion that library staff members essentially profile telephone callers based on their employment status is ludicrous. Garnett seems to suggest that library staff members brush off or hurry along callers (usually female) who appear to be asking for help they don't really need, and instead give their available time to callers (usually male) who are likely too busy to come to the library themselves.

The notion here is that telephone reference is not for everyone—just for busy people who, if they had the time, would certainly present themselves in person at the library. The telephone, it seems, was something to be used only for serious, consequential information needs and not frivolous inquiries such that "club women" might make.

In 1943, an article appeared in the *Library Quarterly* entitled "Do Colleges Need Reference Service?" That the question was even being asked indicates how slow academic libraries were to offer dedicated reference assistance to students. The fallacy had long been established that scholars do not need such assistance, because they were scholars, after all, and should not need it. Fortunately, that circular reasoning began to give way after this article appeared. The author, Lulu Ruth Reed, a graduate of the University of Chicago Library School, makes clear in a detailed study of undergraduates that students were ill-equipped to do research without assistance when they started college, and did not gain significantly in the ability by the time they were seniors. Reed summed up her findings in a series of terse statements that indicate without question the need college students have for librarians to provide reference assistance:

- Students have not acquired specific and detailed knowledge of reference tools, such as dictionaries and encyclopedias.
- Students have not learned to associate types of questions with types of books most likely to answer those questions.
- Students have not learned to associate authors or editors with types of material.
- Students have not learned to associate topics with general fields of knowledge and consequently do not benefit, to a maximum degree, by labels indicating divisions of the classification scheme.
- Students have not learned to use parts of books effectively and have inadequate knowledge of bibliographical features such as footnotes, bibliographies, and indexes.
- Student interpretation of specimen entries from [various indexes] reveals inability to understand and locate information by means of these tools.
- Students are not able to evaluate sources of information readily.
- Students do not understand the functions of various library departments.

While discouraging for the undergraduates she studied, Reed's conclusions were definitely encouraging for practitioners of reference services in academic libraries, because they indicated how much the surveyed students (and all of those who followed) need the guidance that reference specialists offer. In addition to making clear just how much college students need help, Reed's article contributed to the growing distinction between what public reference librarians did best (answering questions, steering people to resources, suggesting reading) and what academic reference librarians did best (teaching students how to do research and how to assess the quality of sources).

Reference in the Mid-Twentieth Century

While public library reference staff were distinguishing themselves as the go-to source for questions that could be answered by consulting printed information, university and college librarians had not made much progress toward the current paradigm of providing proactive, specialized research instruction. But reference desks at academic libraries increasingly fielded calls from the public. With a telephone in nearly every household and more people than ever enrolled in college classes across the nation, academic libraries were, like their public-library counterparts, becoming the guides to information outside their immediate zone. However, that solo starring role for librarians as the best and often the only source for information lasted for only a few more decades.

For the most part, reference services happen outside the realm of popular imagination. Few people outside the profession have ever given extensive thought to the process—even library patrons usually stop thinking about the reference desk moments after walking away from it. But in 1945, the concept of librarians providing useful, vital reference assistance was featured prominently in a long *Saturday Evening Post* article entitled "Brain Service for Congress." The author, Lucy Salamanca, invokes the image of a member of Congress citing facts and figures during an argument on the floor. She asks, "Where does your senator or representative get those statistics he is always spouting, that apt quotation from a classic he has never read?" (1945: 17). For seemingly the first time, the general public was asked a question that forced them to think about the need for someone, or some entity, to provide answers and supply information.

The article goes on to discuss the Library of Congress (LOC) Legislative Reference Service, where some "70 professional researchers" were employed. Among them were experts in the fields of sociology, economics, geography, literature, history, political science, and law; requests were handled by the person most knowledgeable in a subject area, rather than by whomever was available at the time. Together, these experts, according to Salamanca, responded to 1,200 to 1,500 reference requests *per month*—and they were not just telling people how to find the bathroom or what time the place closed. They handled constituent inquiries as well, which were not received directly, but passed along from the various offices of senators and representatives. The LOC Legislative Reference Service stands as an early model of professionalism and seriousness for today's public and academic library administrators.

The American public was forced once again to think about reference services when the 1957 film *Desk Set* was released. Katherine Hepburn plays a member of the gigantic (and fictional) Federal Broadcasting Company. Her character, Bunny Watson, is head of the FBC's "Research and Reference" department; she and her all-female staff spend their days primarily on the phone, taking calls from people with fairly simple questions (Are there any poisons that leave no trace? Do Eskimos really rub noses as a greeting? Where is this quotation from? What are the names of Santa's reindeer?) and making calls to track down the answers. The questions they get are fairly easy to answer and fall under the category of "general" reference questions.

The most interesting thing about this film, from the perspective of this book's subject, is that these characters are reference providers outside the context of librarians as book collectors and protectors. The staff of Watson's department deal in information services only; they have books on their desks and on shelves nearby, which presumably they consult, but they also sometimes answer questions without looking anything up. Peg Costello, played by Joan Blondell, is the baseball expert—taking a call about batting averages, she can recite the numeric details of Ty Cobb's career with confidence and ease. And Watson can recite chunks of Longfellow's "Song of Hiawatha" while searching her office for something. And yet as smart as she is, Watson is just a step or two above the classic "old maid librarian" portrayal. Much of the first half of the film concerns her rather sad and unsuccessful attempts to snag a rising male executive (actually her boss)—she even wears her hair in the stereotypical librarian bun.

Into the well-ordered and successful information-providing enclave at FBC comes a disruptor: Richard Sumner, played by Spencer Tracy. He's a "methods engineer" (i.e., an efficiency expert) for the corporation, and plans to revamp the reference department by installing a computer that will answer reference questions. Soon the ladies are all pink-slipped by the new payroll computer. Meanwhile, Sumner's new machine (named

EMERAC—Electromagnetic **ME**mory and **R**esearch **A**rithmetical **C**alculator), after an initial apparent success, proves incapable of handling nuanced questions despite its loud, busy clicking and patterns of flashing lights. Bunny Watson mocks the machine's clumsy interpretation of questions and laughs openly as, inevitably, the machine starts spitting out punch cards and giving off smoke. Everything ends happily, though, when the payroll situation is sorted out (no one was supposed to be fired). Sumner learns a lesson about the value of human input in reference services, and Watson learns a lesson about the value of computerized input in same. And in those two lessons, the future was born.

The film initially appears to reduce the human/computer equation to a false dichotomy: you either have humans answering reference questions, or you have a computer. Of course, the story makes clear that no such thing was ever intended—EMERAC was installed to supplement the humans, not replace them—just as it makes clear that completely automating the payroll department is a major mistake. In the end, *Desk Set* tells us, humans and machines need each other, and do a better job working together than working apart. It's all played for smiles, but the idea that computers would lead to a reduced workforce was no laughing matter to American society in the 1950s. Many articles on the subject appeared in the short-lived magazine, *The American Socialist* (1954–1959), and history shows clearly that as automation has expanded, human operators have become less necessary. Soon, perhaps, even cars will not need people to operate them.

◎ Modern Reference Services

By the 1960s, computers had changed the paradigm for librarians much as the telephone had done several decades earlier. Room-sized machines like that shown in *Desk Set* gave way, thanks to rapid developments in microcircuitry, to ever-smaller machines that could do ever-increasing complex tasks and store more data. After the shrinking of data storage made possible by the microcircuit, changes were steady and rapid in all types of libraries, and librarians' jobs changed as well. Given the expansion of library holdings, both in print and electronic form, many reference providers found themselves doing more and more research instruction in addition to the traditional answering of questions.

In 1964, Katharine G. Harris addressed the developing trends in reference services within public libraries. She noted that in recent decades, the primary role of the librarian had shifted from dealing with *books* to dealing with *information*. Public libraries had already become "information centers" within their communities. She also commented on the growing number of adults pursuing postsecondary education after the end of World War II, and the way people all across the nation had become interested in world affairs through the increasingly sophisticated content on television. A more intellectually curious populace, she reasoned, needed reliable reference assistance and sources. She pointed out that the greatest change since those early decades after the founding of the ALA and *Library Journal* involved a movement from the "purely literary demands" made of library staff members (book suggestions, reading assistance) to inquiries springing out of "educational, vocational, and business needs" (383). A small public library even in 1964 simply could not fulfill every information request with its limited resources, so Harris encouraged cooperation and what today is called "partnering" among institutions.

By the late 1960s, reference was subjected to a more scientific approach, as exemplified by William A. Katz in his first edition of *Introduction to Reference Work*. This 1969 publication, which many in public-services librarianship first encountered in subsequent editions as a library school textbook, offered a new way to think about reference. Most strikingly, Katz included flowcharts that showed the reference process from multiple perspectives, and established the precedent of quantifying not only the number of transactions, but the nature of those interactions. Katz's approach caught on, and later writings about reference services tended to follow his numerical and diagrammatical example. This emphasis encouraged the professionalization of reference assistance.

Phone technology had earlier transformed the way library staff handled inquiries. With the advent of phone lines, the volume of questions drastically increased, because the staff still had people in the library asking questions, and now they faced the possibility of the phone ringing whenever they weren't on another call. By the early 1970s, though, reference providers had become accustomed to, and even proficient at, prioritizing phone calls while dealing with patrons face to face. But as figure 1.2 indicates, reference transactions were still conducted primarily in person, when a patron approached a labeled desk.

Almost as if on cue, another technology arrived to complicate the lives of librarians working with the public: email. The earliest email messaging programs began in the early 1960s, but not until the early 1980s did the widespread use of LANs (local area networks) allow the linking of personal computers, and thus make email the communication phenomenon it still is. The technical history of email is complicated, but its impact on libraries was steadily felt throughout the 1980s.

Figure 1.2. Duke University's Perkins Library reference desk, c. 1975. https://www.flickr.com/photos/dukeyearlook/5497146749. *Source:* Duke University Archives, box 65 (UAPC-065-019-006)

According to Cordell (2013), email sent to libraries in these early days on college campuses tended to ask about specific library services like photocopying, checkout policies, renewals, and so on. In other words, students weren't asking complicated questions or initiating research instruction via email—they were just getting answers to simple questions. In 1992, Ann Bristow attempted to codify email reference services and lay out a plan that distinguished it from handling in-person or telephone inquiries. Most important, she described the limits of email transactions, which often require several messages back and forth before the information sought is clearly established. Questions were also raised as to how often library staff would check emails, who would bear principal responsibility for answering them, for how long and in what manner the questions and answers should be stored, how these transactions were to be counted in the daily statistics, and whether reference supervisors would monitor exchanges.

Later publications further analyzed the place and nature of email reference transactions. In 1996, Eileen G. Abels expressed the opinion that an actual reference interview (what needs to take place before a question can be answered) via email requires three separate messages:

- A "problem statement" from the library user who initiates the transaction (i.e., an inquiry)
- A response from the library-based reference services provider (i.e., a summary and/or follow-up to the inquiry)
- A confirmation from the user of that summary, and/or additional details relating to the inquiry

And all of that needs to take place before the message or messages containing the response to the actual inquiry can be sent. Clearly, email reference was here to stay, but it was proving to be more labor-intensive than communication in person or even on the telephone. Still, it had (and still has) real advantages. For one thing, large amounts of detailed information can be conveyed in an email that would be difficult to capture in a conversation. The sender can take time with it—check it over for accuracy, and even rewrite parts of it. A copy of questions and replies can be saved, and the information used later in another email or report. Also, and vitally for library administrators, an email message can be preserved and analyzed later in a way that out-loud conversations cannot be.

In 1978, Katz published a new edition of his *Introduction to Reference Work*. His chapter on computer-assisted reference services made clear that the days when computers ruled the school were still a long way off. Computers were still exotic in 1978, and it was rare for a library to actually own one. Instead, libraries made use of computer services that accepted search requests. Public libraries were even farther behind the curve on the integration of computer technology, but they did make progress during the 1980s. By the 1990s, library catalogs were being digitized across the nation, and the new CD-ROM periodical indexes had appeared. Card catalogs still dominated library space, but the information once contained only in heavy printed books was now available in smaller and smaller packages, in CD-ROMs, online databases and catalogs, and (by the mid-1990s) a vigorous and rapidly expanding Internet. For users confronted with this sometimes dizzying array of options, research instruction became essential.

Despite the rapid progress in the quality of reference services over the past century, some library professionals were dissatisfied. In "Library Reference Service: An Unrecognized Crisis—A Symposium," Peter Hernon and Charles R. McClure (1987) wrote that unobtrusive surveys had revealed a serious problem with reference: providers regularly and demonstrably did not provide quality assistance to patrons. Far too often, they gave inaccurate answers to questions, seemed unfamiliar with basic reference publications, conducted superficial reference interviews, gave too few referrals to other libraries or librarians, and displayed inadequate searching skills. Their dismal findings, which the authors said applied to both public and academic libraries, triggered a series of replies and rebuttals. A large number of library school instructors and deans weighed in to discuss how to improve this vitally important part of library service. Some of the same problems still exist today; in fact, the kind of service described by Hernon and McClure is something of a default: if reference providers get inadequate or insufficient training, that's exactly how they will do the job—poorly.

In 1995, two employees of Minnesota's St. Cloud State University, Keith Ewing and Robert Hauptman, dropped a bomb into the sedate world of academic librarianship. In "Is Traditional Reference Service Obsolete?" they went much farther than Hernon and McClure and said flat out that reference services in higher education should simply be eliminated rather than constantly rethought and reconfigured. They claimed that most reference interactions were merely directional, or required the simplest of answers. Anyone with a high school diploma, they said, could do the job: "It does not require any special educational preparation to direct a student or faculty member to a particular library department, a photocopier, a lavatory, or a general almanac" (1995: n.p.). Fortunately for those in the profession, there was an immediate and forceful push-back against Ewing and Hauptman's provocative thesis, and it was generally rejected by many library professionals. Following that article, repeated cases were made in the mid-1990s for the importance of professional-level reference assistance at university libraries.

One librarian who has had a great deal of influence on the nature of technology training, including how it applies to reference work, is Anne Grodzins Lipow. Long affiliated with University of California–Berkeley, Lipow began a consulting and publishing service, Library Solutions Institute and Press, after her retirement in 1991. It has published many titles relating to libraries, including one called *Rethinking Reference in Academic Libraries* (1993), which developed out of a workshop on the topic. One presenter at the workshop, Jerry D. Campbell, suggested it was time for some new terminology. Instead of "reference service providers," Campbell suggested calling them "access engineers," because they typically spend a good portion of their time helping users get to the right information—which printed sources or databases to use, what passwords to input, and so on. Though the term failed to take off, Campbell's focus accurately captured a primary role for reference providers. In addition to discussing and facilitating access with patrons, reference desk workers are often the first to notice when access problems arise and the first to notify administrators of the problem.

When the web browser Mosaic was released in 1993, followed by Netscape in 1994, library users and information providers alike experienced the most radical change since the telephone. Suddenly, vast amounts of information were available online, and the quantity was growing daily. The availability of all that information outside of printed books (most of which were in libraries) prompted questions about whether librarians and their dusty books were now unnecessary, a relic of a past paradigm that had been replaced. But librarians were learning right alongside the patrons—navigating the Internet, joining listservs and user groups, grappling with online databases, and developing ways to help patrons assess the value of reference resources. Quantity became a new problem: with so many resources, how did the user know which one was the best? With library users needing more assistance than ever before, questions about whether librarians were even necessary were ignored by most members of the profession.

During the late 1990s and early 2000s, users in both public and academic libraries were confronted with additional methods for contacting reference providers. In addition to an in-person visit, a phone call, or an email, users now had the option of connecting via chat technology, text messaging, Skype, and social networking. These new methods proved especially popular with high school students and undergraduates, some of whom might not have bothered to make contact using more traditional means. By establishing multiple avenues of access, especially for younger users, library reference administrators ensure that even those individuals who have never set foot in the library can get access to help.

The need to revisit and rethink reference services will never end. As Jack O'Gorman and Barry Trott note in their 2009 article, "What Will Become of Reference in Academic and Public Libraries?" users with newly acquired access to electronic information via the Internet were relying more and more on those sources, despite the availability of higher-quality and more authoritative information in printed books. Those users also, said the authors, "think Wikipedia is the font of all human knowledge" (327).

The problem of addressing users' assumption that "everything is online" is a familiar one for all public-services librarians, and somewhat of a Catch-22: if the users won't contact us because they think they don't need to, how can we help them understand the intrinsic and important differences in the quality of information? O'Gorman and Trott's article came out before there was much overlap between electronic and printed information—today the dilemma is even more complex, because we access print-original information like full-text articles via the Internet, so it's not advisable to condemn online sources without distinguishing which ones are better. Rather, reference providers must commit to perpetually (and patiently) explaining the difference between *print-original* (costly to produce, so has usually gone through an editing and fact-checking process) and *web-original* information (not costly, so often goes straight from the creators' mind to being "published" online).

As is clear from this chronological survey of reference developments over the past (roughly) 130 years, the library profession will always involve providing reference assistance, but how that help is given will no doubt continue to evolve. Since the year the American Library Association was founded and Samuel Swett Green established the importance of a proactive approach, patrons have made use of an ever-increasing array of options for contacting someone who can help them with an information search. As those options developed, the nature of the librarians' job was shifting slowly but surely from "a mere custodian of materials to a highly personal and knowledgeable assistant to users" (Deng, 2014: 260). In the Internet era, with information available in quantities that threaten to drown the inexperienced seeker of information, library staff who can help those seekers discern the differences in quality are more necessary than ever, though not necessarily in person. Reference can be provided without the seeker and provider ever meeting, speaking, or learning each other's names. At one time, assistance was available only by approaching a formidable wooden desk staffed by equally formidable individuals (as shown earlier in figure 1.1); today's library-located reference desks tend to be lower and have nearby chairs for longer discussions and help sessions. Figure 1.3 shows a modern reference desk.

Figure 1.3.   The reference desk at Santa Rosa Junior College. https://libraries.santarosa.edu/doyletour2. *Photograph courtesy of Santa Rosa Junior College Libraries*

◉ Key Points

This chapter has provided a look at the history of reference services, which has been, without question, a success story in which those charged with providing service in libraries have met the challenges of each new social and technological development. In particular,

- Reference services have existed for as long as people have collected information.
- ALA's Reference and User Services Association (RUSA) is the entity that officially defines "reference work" for librarians; its last official definition was created in 2008.
- Since the late nineteenth century, the primary role of the librarian has evolved steadily: from custodian of printed materials, to reading advisor, to provider of simple answers, and, finally, to partners in complex research inquiries and projects.
- The steady development of communication and data storage technologies has profoundly affected the work of reference services providers: first the telephone, then the microchip, then email and, latest but not last, "virtual" communication via chat and Skype. Research instruction is an important, if not always openly practiced, part of reference services.

The next chapter is about reference collections: resources both print and electronic, and the place and importance of research guides and other instruction materials.

⊚ References

Abels, Eileen G. 1996. "The E-mail Reference Interview." *Reference Quarterly* 35, no. 3 (Spring): 345–58.

Bishop, William Warner. 1915. "The Theory of Reference Work." *Bulletin of the American Library Association* 9, no. 4: 134–39. Accessed via Hathi Trust, www.hathitrust.org.

Bristow, Ann. 1992. "Academic Reference Service over Electronic Mail." *College & Research Libraries News* 53, no. 10 (November): 631–32, 637.

Campbell, Jerry D. 1993. "In Search of New Foundations for Reference." In *Rethinking Reference in Academic Libraries*, edited by Anne Grodzins Lipow, 3–14. Berkeley, CA: Library Solutions Press.

Cordell, Roseanne M. 2013. *Library Reference Services and Information Literacy: Models for Academic Institutions.* Hershey, PA: IGI Global.

Davidson, Charles. 1898. "Use and Abuse of Aid in Research." *Library Journal* 23 (August): 140–45.

Deng, Liya. 2014. "The Evolution of Library Reference Services: From General to Special, 1876–1920s." *Libri: International Journal of Libraries & Information Services* 64, no. 3 (September): 254–62.

Ewing, Keith, and Robert Hauptman. 1995. "Is Traditional Reference Service Obsolete?" *Journal of Academic Librarianship* 21, no. 1: 3–6.

Fletcher, William Isaac. 1894. *Public Libraries in America.* Boston: Roberts Brothers. Accessed via Archive.org, https://archive.org/stream/publiclibraries00fletgoog#page/n0/mode/2up.

Garnett, Emily. 1936. "Reference Service by Telephone." *Library Journal* 61, no. 21 (December): 909–11.

Green, Samuel Swett. 1876. "Personal Relations Between Librarians and Readers." *Library Journal* 1, no. 1 (October): 74–81. Reprinted in the June 15, 1993, issue of *Library Journal*, S4–S5.

Harris, Katharine G. 1964. "Reference Service in Public Libraries." *Library Trends* 12, no. 3: 373–89.

Hernon, Peter, and Charles R. McClure. 1987. "Library Reference Service: An Unrecognized Crisis—A Symposium." *Journal of Academic Librarianship* 13, no. 2: 69–80.

Houston, Anne M. 2016. "What's in a Name? Toward a New Definition of Reference." *Reference and User Services Quarterly* 55, no. 3 (Spring): 186–88.

Kabir, Abulfazal. 2003. "Ranganathan: A Universal Librarian." *Journal of Educational Media & Library Sciences* 40, no. 4 (June): 453–59.

Kaplan, Louis. 1964. "The Early History of Reference Service in the United States." *Library Review* 11, no. 3: 286–90.

Katz, William A. 1969. *Introduction to Reference Work.* New York: McGraw Hill.

———. 1978. *Introduction to Reference Work.* Third edition. New York: McGraw Hill.

O'Gorman, Jack, and Barry Trott. 2009. "What Will Become of Reference in Academic and Public Libraries?" *Journal of Library Administration* 49, no. 4: 327–39.

Reed, Lulu Ruth. 1943. "Do Colleges Need Reference Service?" *Library Quarterly* 13, no. 3 (July): 232–40.

Renfrew, Colin. 2008. *Prehistory: The Making of the Human Mind.* New York: Modern Library.

Salamanca, Lucy. 1945. "Brain Service for Congress." *Saturday Evening Post* 217, no. 28 (January 6): 17, 72.

Wyer, James I. 1930. *Reference Work: A Textbook for Students of Library Work and Librarians.* Chicago: American Library Association. Accessed via Hathi Trust, www.hathitrust.org.

Reference Collections Today

SAMUEL JOHNSON, ACCORDING TO HIS FRIEND and biographer John Boswell (1791), said that there are two kinds of knowing: "We know a subject ourselves, or we know where we can find information upon it." And if anyone knew something about knowing, it was Johnson. His contributions to English literature are many, and include the first great dictionary of the English language in 1755. Completing that massive work took Johnson nine years, and certainly he learned a great deal during the process about the difference between knowing something oneself and knowing how to find it out. In her essay, "Dr. Burney's Evening Party," Virginia Woolf said about Johnson, "the resources of his own mind . . . were huge" (1932: 111). In fact, Johnson completed his dictionary without much outside help apart from a large collection of literary works, which he mined for quotations and definitions. Even the great Dr. Johnson, it seems, needed a reference library.

ⓢ The Know-It-All Stereotype

Librarians throughout history have frequently been mistaken for know-it-alls, in part because members of the profession have encouraged that portrayal. In the second issue of *Library Journal* (then called the *American Library Journal*), Lloyd P. Smith wrote, "A librarian should not only be a walking catalogue, but a living cyclopedia." Furthermore, he noted, "Librarians . . . are expected to know everything; and in one sense they should know everything" (1876: 70). A few years later, the same journal published an unattributed piece, labeled simply "from the *London Times*," which stated, "The ideal librarian must be a man of rare and almost superhuman gifts" ("The Ideal Librarian," 1882: 106).

Most public services librarians today admittedly do tend to know quite a lot, but few would care to be held to that early standard promoted by *LJ*. Fortunately, the pressure didn't last. By 1936, Harriet E. Howe informed potential members of the profession that near-omniscience was *not* actually a requirement for the job in *Library Quarterly*. Instead, she wrote, the ideal candidate for professional librarianship has three qualities: (1) broad subject knowledge with some specialization; (2) library-school training; and (3) personal traits such as initiative, imagination, and interest in people. Howe stressed the importance of "emotional stability" over encyclopedic mental access to facts and figures, and a generation of librarians breathed a sigh of relief.

Yet the image of the all-knowing reference librarian persisted in popular culture. As noted in chapter 1, the 1957 film *Desk Set* features a group of bright women who run a research and reference department for a media corporation. But rather than show these women spending time consulting reference books and crafting qualified, source-based responses to the people who contact them, the filmmakers preferred to show off their near-omniscience on selected topics such as baseball and poetry. What's missing in the portrayal is the commonsense notion that a reference provider can be highly effective at the job without having anything close to the total recall of trivia that the *Desk Set* characters display. While public services librarians might celebrate the fact that an entire film was once made about their occupation, they might also question the decision to present reference types as know-it-alls.

The stereotype is even more prevalent on the page, especially in mystery and detective novels. Librarians, at least the information services types, regularly show up in that genre because they either provide information or (more rarely) obscure it. Numerous portrayals of literary librarians are outlined in Grant Burns's *Librarians in Fiction: A Critical Bibliography* (1998), including the sympathetic novice monk William in Umberto Eco's 1983 historical novel, *The Name of the Rose*, set in a medieval monastery. William is not a librarian, but he displays the stereotypical erudition and depth of knowledge associated with that group. Another character tells him, "What a magnificent librarian you would have been . . . you know everything" (567). Once again, it seems, the defining characteristic for a librarian is a claim to omniscience. In fact, the librarians in Eco's book are hardly heroic by modern standards—they spend more time blocking potential users of printed books than they do helping them gain access.

Apart from imagined characters in films and historical novels, were actual librarians throughout history assumed to be freakishly well informed? Probably not. Professional librarians today are generally well informed and educated, and bookish types have always been drawn to the business, but the know-it-all is, thankfully, a rare breed in the real world.

Yet the stereotype has persisted for centuries. In 1901, John Ashhurst, a librarian at the Free Library of Philadelphia, explained how the omniscient librarian image came about. He wrote that the librarian of his day was "treated with a certain amount of deference" if he proved able to answer questions frequently without looking anything up (268). Maybe. Or maybe, as the mages and wizards do in medieval worlds of fantasy writers, people just need someone to know things in a world filled with frightening unknowables.

So the stereotype exists, but does it reflect the reality of information provision in libraries? Are inquiring patrons really getting accurate and concise information from reference providers who simply know the answers without checking sources? That's not an easy question to answer, but apparently not. For the past three decades, library science professionals have been arguing about what is called the "55 percent rule," which was established by researchers Peter Hernon and Charles R. McClure. In a 1986 issue of *Library Journal*, Hernon and McClure published an article entitled "Unobtrusive Reference Testing: The 55 Percent Rule." They found, through unobtrusive testing (i.e., the subjects did not know they were being tested) at libraries in eight cities, that information providers answered questions correctly only 55 percent of the time.

The conclusions of Hernon and McClure have been revisited many times since 1986, and their methodology has been questioned as well (see especially Bailey, 1987; Durrance, 1989; Jardine, 1995; and Hubbertz, 2007). They also found that library staff members at reference points did several other things wrong: they made insufficient referral to library services, they failed to conduct reference interviews effectively, and they deployed ineffective search strategies when consulting resources. In all, Hernon and McClure painted a sad picture of reference services at the libraries subjected to their study. If those reference providers were even a little bit typical of people in that position, then clearly there is no basis (and probably never has been) for the stereotype of the librarian as a know-it-all. So what created this persistent, though mythical, image?

Beth Posner offered an intriguing answer. In her 2002 article, "Know-it-All Librarians," Posner lays out the case for why no reasonable person would ever want to be painted that way. Children are routinely told that "no one likes a know-it-all," and in adults the delusion of omniscience is considered a "clear sign of psychological dysfunction" (114). And clearly, the desire to know everything didn't do Adam and Eve any good. The same is true for Faust, the figure of German legend who sold the devil his soul so that he could achieve omniscience. Even in our modern society, asks Posner, don't we find know-it-alls "quite annoying"? In fact, she adds, displaying a know-it-all attitude runs counter to the American Library Association's established code of ethics for librarians. The code calls for a "courteous response to all requests"—the opposite of what a know-it-all attitude conveys (http://www.ala.org/advocacy/proethics/codeofethics/codeethics).

For another example of the imperious, know-everything librarian, check out the famous library scene in the 1982 film, *Sophie's Choice*. It shows Polish immigrant Sophie, as played by Meryl Streep, crossing an ornate and columned library foyer that wouldn't be out of place in a house of worship. She approaches the information desk and tentatively addresses the male clerk. She asks, in halting English, for help finding a catalog listing for the nineteenth-century American poet "Emile Dickens." Any normal reference desk staffer would know what she meant, but the arrogant dolt behind the desk does not: "You won't find any such listing . . . Charles Dickens in an English writer. There is no American poet by the name of Dickens." Sophie pushes back, insisting that there is such a poet, and he verbally attacks her. Then she faints.

The portrayal is obviously over-the-top, but why does it exist at all? Perhaps it has something to do with the very nature of libraries as places where knowledge resides, and the need for patrons to approach a desk staffed by busy-looking people. Every information provider has heard patrons begin their interaction by apologizing for interrupting or for asking a "stupid question." Whatever the reason for the know-it-all stereotype, it exists, and must be countered with real information from library professionals.

Posner (2002) offers this breakdown of what public-services librarians actually *do* tend to know:

- How to find and evaluate information (different from knowing facts)
- How to collect, preserve, organize, and dispense information
- How to get things done (e.g., troubleshoot copy machines, load microfilm readers, manage staff)
- How to work with people (including difficult or stressed-out people)
- How to impart information literacy (i.e., teaching others how to find what they want to know)
- How to work effectively with both electronic and print information (even user-unfriendly sources)

All of these knowledge skills are far more important than knowing simple facts à la *Desk Set*. Posner follows her list of what librarians know with what they can *do* to combat harmful stereotypes:

- *Study the image of their profession.* The stereotypes (know-it-all, spinster, out-of-touch nerd, ivory tower idealist) exist for a reason.
- *Share how librarians find things out.* Represent the profession realistically in every encounter by explaining, clearly and openly, how and why librarians know certain things, and why they do not know other things.
- *Avoid thinking of themselves as "know-nothings."* Yes, the library profession doesn't always get the respect it deserves, but librarians have an earned expertise within the information world, and should embrace that.
- *Study the changing nature of information.* Library science programs should offer more instruction in epistemology. Only librarians who understand the nature of how information changes over time can really understand how to use it.
- *Teach people about the limits of information technology.* Of course, the sum total of knowledge is not on the free Internet—but tell patrons that, repeatedly. Explain why librarians are still necessary.
- *Be proactive in helping people search for information.* Information services professionals do not simply "refer" people to sources the way a grocery store clerk indicates the correct aisle for sugar. Aim at making every patron self-sufficient—teach them the strategies that work.
- *Fight against unnecessary limits.* Fight for what you need in terms of budget, schedule, staff, etc.
- *Accept necessary limits.* Don't push resources (including staff) to the breaking point.
- *Publicize realistic depictions of librarians in fiction and the media.* Celebrate the replacement, wherever you can find it, of negative stereotypes with better images— the librarian as a trained, approachable, personable, and tech-savvy ally inside and outside of the library.

No single librarian is responsible for the existence of the stereotypes, and no one person can combat them. If the stereotypes persist, then the job of overcoming them isn't finished yet.

⊚ Developing a Reference Collection

As anyone who does the job knows, library-based information providers do not simply supply factual answers to any and all questions based on their own encyclopedic knowledge. Instead, they rely on *reference resources*, whether print or electronic. What the inquiring patron needs, therefore, is both the person and the sources—the former uses and interprets the latter on behalf of the patron. The people part of the reference transaction is covered in chapter 3; here, the emphasis is on the resources used by reference providers.

What is a Reference Collection?

Given the complex relationship between print and electronic versions of books and articles, and the relatively high price of dedicated "reference" publications, reference coordinators must make careful choices when deciding on a collection to support reference services.

A reference collection is defined by Evans and Carter as "the information resources selected by the reference staff to do reference work" (2009: 92). In other words, it could be anything the staff finds helpful. Usually a reference collection consists of materials easily accessed by library staff, either print items housed nearby, or material accessed online via the library network or public access. A separate area is almost always used for shelving reference books, and these are generally non-circulating. The handful of resources most frequently used by the reference desk staff may migrate to a "ready reference" shelf, but for the most part, reference books are accessible to anyone in the library. According to Evans and Carter, libraries build reference collections to accomplish three things:

1. To answer the information needs of the library's clientele
2. To facilitate access to the library's collection
3. To provide guidance to information resources beyond the local library collection

And those responsible for setting up and maintaining a reference collection usually operate with written or unwritten guidelines to justify each item. In general, these guidelines consider the following factors:

- *Usefulness in answering reference questions.* This factor is judged according to the experience of the reference staff. The usefulness of an information source depends on the needs of the library's staff and patron base.
- *Depth of coverage.* A work designed to introduce subjects with brief discussions only (e.g., encyclopedias, yearbooks).
- *Local needs.* The recurrence of certain questions can prompt the placement of materials in a reference collection (e.g., a history of the local county) that might otherwise go in the general collection.
- *Format.* Most works added to a reference collection are designed to be consulted rather than read from start to finish (e.g., almanacs, atlases, dictionaries).
- *Frequency of use.* Some materials (like road atlases) end up in a reference collection because they are consulted frequently by patrons and staff alike. Time is saved by keeping such items physically close to the reference desk.

- *Mission of the parent organization.* If the library is connected to a faith-based institution, for example, then appropriate reference materials would relate to the institution's mission. Fine-tuning collection development policies is especially important in special libraries.
- *Expected user groups.* Every library has a unique set of user groups that may expect certain materials or formats in the reference collection. A corporate user group, for example, would expect business-related materials that are as current as possible.

The History of Reference Collections

William A. Katz, in his 1998 book *Cuneiform to Computer: A History of Reference Sources*, traces the history of reference collections back to the origins of writing itself, when scribes in Egypt and Mesopotamia collected information to be consulted later. From that time until the modern age, library books, especially the most useful and most expensive ones, were closely guarded, and in some cases, even chained to library shelves, as in figure 2.1.

That paradigm began to shift in the late nineteenth century, with the founding of the American Library Association and a growing understanding on the part of librarians that open shelves and access to information was a higher priority than protecting books from potential users. But even after most libraries became circulating, some restrictions continued where reference books were concerned—patrons were allowed access, but could not remove those titles from the library. In the late nineteenth century, a Princeton College librarian wrote, "At least a small selection of the best reference books should be accessible to the public" (Richardson, 1896: 977). By the early twentieth century, the proliferation of books designed and used specifically for reference prompted another librarian, Alice Bertha Kroeger, to produce the first book-length guide to those publications (*Guide to the Study and Use of Reference Books: A Manual for Librarians, Teachers and Students*, 1902).

Carol A. Singer (2010) has traced the history of that subset of reference sources usually termed "ready reference," items kept closest to hand by those who provide reference services. According to Singer, the term "ready reference" has been used since at least 1876. For almost 100 years following that label, the ready reference collections in libraries grew and grew, but today, most libraries have shifted those print volumes back to the regular reference collection and rely more on electronic access to information at the reference desk.

The first publication that became a staple of library reference work was almost certainly the *Encyclopedia Britannica*. Initially published in three volumes between 1768 and 1771, this landmark production has continued to the present day. The last printed edition, in 2010, took up 32 volumes; the content has continued to expand in digital form. The *Britannica*'s purpose was clear: to collect basic information and facts covering a wide variety of topics, and to present that information in an accessible, compact form. That's what most general encyclopedias have done ever since.

Since the late eighteenth century, similar publications became available in libraries, but the term "reference book" itself did not take hold until the modern public library developed about 100 years later (Tyckoson, 2011). At that time, librarians began separating out books that people "referred" to or consulted, rather than read from cover to cover, and generally kept these close to where staff members answered patron questions.

Figure 2.1.   The sixteenth-century chained library of Zutphen, in the Netherlands, one of the few such libraries that still exist. http://erikkwakkel.tumblr.com/post/49509415868/the-chained-library-of-zutphen-i-took-these. *Photograph by Dr. Erik Kwakkel, De Librije, Zutphen*

Information wasn't easy to come by for the average citizen, and reference books became quite popular with library users. But their usefulness and relative expense forced libraries to keep such titles non-circulating, and that model has remained common.

Today's library users are far less dependent on consulting printed reference works physically held at a local library, but reference titles are more prevalent and specialized than ever before. As the use of shelved reference titles declines, it seems, with each passing year, staff members who still value their printed collections are encouraged to determine how much use those items get, and to consider allowing them to circulate, albeit with a shorter loan period than the regularly circulating titles.

Selecting Reference Sources

Each library must determine what reference sources are essential to that location and patron base, and ideally will establish a collection development policy for reference sources that outlines whether priority should be given to print or digital versions of selected titles. General considerations for purchasing reference titles include the library's budget for such purchases, and the availability of reference sources in other nearby libraries. Evans and Carter (2009: 93–94) recommend that the following issues be considered when evaluating materials for a reference collection:

- *Demand.* Will anyone ever use this item? Does the cost reflect its value to the library and its users?
- *Aim and scope.* What is the purpose of the work? Does it meet its stated goals? What kind of questions will it answer? Will this work do something different than materials already in the collection, or do something similar, but better?
- *Timeliness.* Is it necessary for a work in this subject field to have the latest information? If this source purports to have the latest information, does it? How is the work updated—for example, by supplements, regular revisions, or new editions, and how often is it updated? If available in multiple formats, which one is more up-to-date?
- *Format.* Is the material arranged logically, whether alphabetically, topically, chronologically, or geographically? Is it easy to use? Are there sufficient cross-references and an index? Is the binding strong enough for heavy use? Is the database interface easy to navigate? Are the graphics of good quality?
- *Authority.* What is the reputation and training of the author or editor? What are the sources of the data? Are they cited in the text? What is the publisher's reputation?
- *Accuracy.* Is the information correct? Is it up-to-date?
- *Alternatives.* When dealing with electronic reference sources, additional concerns must be considered, such as the stability of the site, hardware and software reliability and compatibility, and the availability and usefulness of help files.

Fortunately, selectors have some standard options for finding out what publications are available. New publications are regularly reviewed in journals such as *Choice Reviews, Library Journal, Public Library Journal,* and *School Library Journal,* and journals within specific subject areas usually have a review section as well. Standing orders can also be placed to ensure that new editions of particular reference titles are acquired right away. Likewise, the selector can establish an approval plan, whereby new titles are delivered automatically, and returned or kept after review.

Types of Reference Sources

Any publication can end up on the "reference" shelves, depending on what has proved useful to the staff. But generally speaking, several established types almost always go on reference shelves:

- *Encyclopedias.* These include general titles such as the *Encyclopedia Britannica*, and more specialized titles such as the *Encyclopedia of New Venture Management*.
- *Indexes.* Print versions are sometimes difficult to use because of volume bulk, and are increasingly scarce; examples include *Granger's Index to Poetry* and *Play Index*. And today, few libraries keep print copies of the formerly ubiquitous *Reader's Guide to Periodical Literature* indexes.
- *Handbooks.* Publications in this category are usually specialized rather than general, and on topics that require detailed information within a subject area such as environmental science or comparative religion; e.g., *Handbook of Nursing Diagnosis* and *Handbook of Narrative Analysis*.
- *Biographies.* Scope varies widely within this type—some, such as the *Dictionary of American Biography*, contain extensive entries, while others might contain just a few facts about a person (*Who's Who*). Many are specialized within professions or groups.
- *Dictionaries.* Every library in the United States has at least one print dictionary that offers a guide to the use of English, but many have a variety of specialized dictionaries as well. Large, general dictionaries of English, such as the *Oxford English Dictionary*, are rarely kept in print form anymore; others, such as the narrowly specialized *Dictionary of Cantonese Slang*, will often be found on shelves where the patron base justifies their presence.
- *Almanacs.* Books of facts and figures were once the only source for such information; today that information can be found in a variety of online sources, but almanacs are still useful. This category includes the *World Almanac and Book of Facts*, but specialized titles are also available, such as the *Almanac of New York City*.
- *Bibliographies.* Either a general list of books (*Books in Print*) or a specialized list for a particular subject (e.g., *A Bibliography of William Wordsworth, 1787–1930*).
- *Maps and atlases.* In print, these volumes are larger than almost all other publications, so they are usually kept in on a separate stand in the reference area. Examples include the *Rand McNally Road Atlas*, the *Historical Atlas of Maine*, and the *Gazetteer of Korea*.
- *Directories.* At one time, lists of people and organizations were available only in print form, and no library or household was without a city directory or phone book. Today, that information is easily accessed online and does not require a specialized publication; however, some titles are still useful in print, such as the *Encyclopedia of Associations* and the *College Bluebook*.

As online access to information apart from dedicated publications becomes increasingly more available, the need for these references sources will decrease. However, for libraries with a patron base that consists of people not comfortable with or adept at online searching, keeping a good selection of print reference sources is essential.

Print or Electronic?

Rosanne Cordell notes in her 2014 article, "Optimizing Library Services: Managing the 21st-Century Reference Collection," that despite the rapid development of information freely available on the Internet, reference collections are still vital to reference services. "One cannot," she states, "depend exclusively on open Web searching on-the-fly to provide the highest quality of assistance" (53); reference providers must have at hand "top sources of information" no matter what patron or what question they are dealing with. And these sources on the shelves labeled "Reference" are not merely for directly addressing patron inquiries, says Cordell—they also play a significant role in research instruction. So whether the titles in a reference collection are available in print or accessed electronically, or both, the main thing is for staff and patrons alike to have access to them.

Cordell (2014) has some advice for reference collection managers who are considering whether to purchase new titles in electronic form. Three primary issues should be considered before making those decisions, each with a set of relevant questions:

- *Cost.* Not a straightforward issue, as it usually is with printed titles. Is the initial cost a one-time payment, or a recurring subscription fee?
- *Potential Use.* Books on a shelf are relatively easy to see and use, but electronic titles might be more elusive. Will patrons be able to find and access the electronic titles easily from their phones and tablets? If the titles are purchased for an academic library, the teaching faculty should be asked whether they will continue to require use of a particular reference work if it is available only in electronic form.
- *Format.* The "interface" for printed books has developed over the last several centuries to the point where the experience of opening and consulting a print volume is a generally positive one. Unfortunately, the same cannot be said for electronic presentations. Is a full-screen view available? Can a range of pages be copied and printed? Can the text be searched? Is the font and type size appropriate and accessible? Can an individual patron create and save notes?

Whatever decision is made, says Cordell, remember to put the emphasis for patrons on the *content*, rather than the *format*, of a reference source. Reference managers must navigate all formats with equal ease and aim at helping users find the best sources, regardless of format.

The Internet Myth

Today's reference providers face an uphill and seemingly never-ending battle against a Goliath called "the Internet." No one can work a reference desk for long without encountering a perception on the part of many patrons that somehow, somewhere, everything is on the Internet. For some, the library is a place different from "the Internet"—the secondary choice for an information search after an online search attempt has failed.

For those in the information services business, the perceived dichotomy between "the library" and "online" is frustrating. In university libraries, reference desk staffers run into that one all the time. Students regularly "confess" that they have not needed the library up until now, because they usually find everything online. Over and over, it is explained to these students that the library's many resources are online, including some the student has already tried. To combat this false dichotomy, library staff members who teach research instruction classes would do well to offer a quick overview of the difference between what can be found via Google, and what is available via the library's network. What follows in the rest of this subsection is a suggested presentation of that difference.[1]

Librarians today operate fully within the wired world. A novelist or journalist might opt to use an old manual typewriter, but no researcher today can get along without online resources such as catalogs, databases, and digital files, and no librarian works apart from those resources. In the prewired era, researchers consulted large, printed indexes in libraries and archives. Today, indexes are accessed almost completely online, and researchers on any subject must get comfortable in that environment. Even sophisticated researchers, however, sometimes do not recognize the differences among types of online information. Essentially, the web is divided between public and subscription access information, which have distinct differences.

Public access information is what you get with a Google search. It is available to anyone who has a wired or wireless connection and a device—no passwords or fees required. For example, a Google search on "Barack Obama" retrieves millions of web pages. Those pages could be anything—government or organizational sites, news pages such as CNN or Fox News, individual blogs, online stores, and so forth. In short, you get a mixed bag of information types. Some of these sites might lead you to pages that require a password and payment; those pages are doorways to *subscription access* information, which is behind a wall of sorts and virtually invisible to someone who does not seek it out. Behind that wall, and millions of others like it, is the "invisible web"—the area of the Internet not uncovered in a Google search. Table 2.1 summarizes the general differences between public and subscription access.

Public access information is free; subscription access information usually requires payment and registration. You can search Google and get results for no charge, but if you search the *New Yorker*'s portal as a non-subscriber, you will get only partial information until you pay for subscriber privileges. Pornography sites operate much the same way: they give away some content in the public access "foyer" of their site, and then offer the user access to much, much more—at a price. Those sites exist to sell a product, which, in the case of pornography, is the same product sold in printed form. It is a business model that dominates the online world—the "good stuff" is often behind a paywall, much as the good stuff in a pharmacy is usually behind the counter.

It is almost as easy to create public access information as it is to find it. Anybody with a minimum of know-how can create web pages, and there are few rules governing content. The Internet operates according to the rules of anarchy; no one polices it. The creators of public access content must not infringe on a copyright, misuse a trademark, or commit libel—other than that, content can be anything its creator desires. No one can

Table 2.1. General Differences between Public and Subscription Sources

PUBLIC ACCESS	SUBSCRIPTION ACCESS
Free or no registration	Usually costs or requires registration
Mixed information types	Single information types
Usually does not go through the traditional editing process	Usually goes through the traditional editing process
Web original	Print original

stop a person from creating an official-looking "Librarians of America" site, even if the creator is not a librarian and says incorrect things about librarianship. This information, because it is both created and accessed with no restrictions, has no filter—it can go from the mind of the creator to the eyes of the researcher with no one saying, "Wait a minute, let's check that before it goes out."

Because of the technology that enables its creation, public access online information is almost 100 percent *web original*: created online to appear online, and thus completely bypassing the print stage. Unlike public access web pages, however, subscription access sources such as newspaper and magazine articles have been, until recent years, almost 100 percent *print original*: they appeared first in print and only subsequently (or simultaneously) appeared online. Today, some online peer-reviewed journals have no print counterpart, but they go through the same review process that a publication intended for print does and are, for the purposes of this chapter, part of the *print original* category. Printed material is certainly susceptible to bias and error but, on the whole, it usually involves more eyes on the text than what has been created specifically for online consumption. For the past few decades, much available print-original information has been digitized and made searchable. By the end of 2013, Google—as part of an ambitious project to digitize every known book—had accomplished the scanning of over 30 million titles, most of them in the public domain and thus not subject to copyright restrictions.

Exceptions aside, the difference is not merely one of format, but quality—in general, a print-original article has gone through the editing process; its web-original counterpart has not. For an article to appear in print, the writer must submit it to an editor. The editor might accept it, but require changes to the text; the article might need to be peer reviewed, and the editor usually checks facts and verifies sources. Also, minor errors in the text are corrected. By the time a piece appears in print, it has been through a filtering process. Web-original publications, by contrast, are subjected to no such filtering. The Internet is full of expressed opinions in blogs, articles, and personal sites; anyone who has anything to say can find a forum online. Many of those same individuals, however, probably could not get their words into print. In brief, the dichotomy between print and electronic versions is irrelevant when the question is access, but when the question is origin, then it matters a great deal.

The Case for Maintaining a Print Collection

While published books are still doing a healthy business, the printed editions of those titles are growing less popular as libraries move toward offering online-only access to many selections. In fact, some libraries with collections focused on the sciences have completely done away with printed books housed at the library building; Florida Polytechnic University, for example, introduced an entirely bookless library several years ago (Riley, 2014), while the University of Michigan's $55 million renovation of the Taubman Health Sciences Library included sending all paper materials to off-site storage (Freed, 2015).

But most general collections still need to maintain a print reference collection. For one thing, says Naomi Lederer (2016), printed reference books reflect a long history of thinking about design and ease of access. The table of contents, the index, the page numbers, the page headers, and the graphics all help make a printed reference book easy to use and to cite. Electronic versions of the same title may or may not contain those useful design elements. Lederer offers the following list for justifying a continued presence for printed reference works:

- *Convenience.* The "hassle factor" favors print over electronic; a printed book is simply easier to access and to use regularly.
- *Jump-off point.* Paging through a printed reference book allows the researcher who starts with almost no information to identify associated details (names, places, dates, topics) almost immediately. Such "paging" is more difficult to do in electronic format.
- *Serendipity and discovery.* You cannot see as much at one time with an e-book, but with a printed book you can take in associated subjects and concepts both directly and peripherally. Flipping through pages leads to more possibilities, so browsing a print edition offers a far greater chance of "stumbling across something new and intriguing" (311).
- *Cost.* Electronic access to quality reference sources is expensive, sometimes prohibitively so. As the cost of e-books rises, libraries on a tight budget would be wiser to invest in print copies of standard reference works, the prices of which tend to be more stable. Print editions, unlike electronic ones, do not require maintenance fees, and offer the option of paying for new editions rather than the requirement of doing so. The usual practice for publishers of online editions is to make the current one unavailable if a new edition has been issued; the library either pays for the update, or loses its access. Weighing up-front costs against ongoing costs is essential.
- *Availability.* Reference collections should include useful printed works that have no electronic counterpart, if they are useful to the patron base.
- *Online irritants.* Most printed books are user-friendly. Software interfaces, however, vary widely on this point. Most people in the library world are familiar with the tendency of electronic resource providers to make changes to their software in the name of improvement, but such changes can create problems for users accustomed to certain functions and layouts. Frequent changes to online resources is a "major irritant" (314), and the lack of a uniform way to mark one's place in a reference work means they cannot be used the way printed volumes can be. Finally, online access is subjected to myriad disruptions: service might go down, the publisher might be updating its site, a hacker might have interfered, etc. These issues do not occur with printed volumes.
- *Use.* In addition to being easier to use in general, printed volumes are easier for visually impaired people to use with help such as a magnifier. And some library users are simply uncomfortable using a mouse and screen to access information; even some younger patrons prefer printed copies to online access. Also, computer terminals and laptops at many libraries are all in use during busy hours, so a student or patron who doesn't bring in a personal device must wait for an open station in order to access electronic titles. A printed reference volume, on the other hand, is available unless someone else is holding it.
- *Historical research.* Some printed sources contain information and references not available in electronic form. Extensive research done 100 years ago, for example, might be presented in a printed reference book that looks outdated, but contains a compilation of facts that would be lost if the volume were withdrawn. There are many examples of such works in genealogy and theater studies, to name just two of many possible subjects. For example, the 1950 publication, *The Parisian Stage: Alphabetical Indexes of Plays and Authors* by Charles B. Wicks, does not have an electronic equivalent. The information might be contained in some other publication, but keeping this print resource despite its advanced age means maintaining

access to a compilation of data that would be difficult to recreate today. Similarly, the 1930 publication, *Index to Printed Virginia Genealogies* by Robert A. Stewart and William G. Stanard, is a standard reference work for doing research on Virginia family history. A limited view is available in Google Books, but interested users outside of a few academic libraries must track down a print version if they want the information it contains.

Format doesn't matter as much as content, obviously, but it does matter—and reference collection managers should think carefully about the issues Lederer raises before deciding to do away with printed materials for the reference desk. But electronic access to reference resources is here to stay, so the following section offers a practical look at working with them.

⑥ Managing Electronic Reference Resources

To one degree or another, all aspects of reference services have been transformed in recent decades. While face-to-face and phone interactions may still be the norm, the use of email, texting, instant chat, social media, and other methods of communication are all on the rise. The physical form of reference services has changed—if a reference desk exists at all in a modern library, it is often configured in a more open and less intimidating way than the massive wooden fortresses encountered by previous generations of reference users. Even the behavior of reference librarians has changed, with a welcoming, supportive approach replacing the shushing of the past.

No area of reference services has undergone a more drastic transformation, however, than reference resources—the materials used by librarians and researchers to answer the most basic questions about virtually every research topic. These changes take many forms and have come about for a variety of reasons, but of all the changes to reference resources, the most important by a wide margin is the proliferation of materials in electronic format.

The digitization of information was among the first of many qualities that popularized personal computers, and later the Internet. From near the beginning of the personal computer era, users could load searchable files into their computers containing information on many subjects—sports statistics, historical events, pricing for various collectibles, and many types of scientific data. Soon, CD-ROMs and Internet sites offered access to so many types of information and data that it appeared to many that the collective knowledge of the human race was somehow stuffed into personal computers. People could find information that had long been available only through books, archived newspapers, and periodicals, all at their fingertips. As early as the 1980s, groundbreaking systems like LexisNexis and InfoTrac offered well-organized access to news, information, and journal articles—albeit for a substantial fee that was beyond the reach of most individual users. These systems were often provided through private and public institutions to their member users. The popularity of such systems encouraged a flood of newcomers, which has continued until today with current leaders like EBSCO, JSTOR, and ProQuest.

The popularity of these new systems further encouraged the perception that the Internet and its resources had made paper library resources obsolete—a fifteenth-century format needlessly taking up valuable space in the era of technology, some said. This controversy continues to the present time, a now decades-long debate concerning the relative merits of paper and electronic library resources. The paper supporters point out the value of serendipitous discovery while browsing paper resources (such as Massis, 2011). They believe the traditional methods are still the best, and cite studies showing that users prefer paper resources (such as Mizrachi, 2015). There is, in fact, often an unspoken implication that paper resources are altogether more scholarly and dignified than their digital usurpers (Terrell, 2015).

The research data on print and electronic format preferences are, however, contradictory. Fans of digital library resources note an overall preference for electronic formats (Ji, Michaels, and Waterman, 2014; Skipton and Bail, 2014) and deeper connections made by students when reading digital materials (Lopatovska and Sessions, 2016). To claims of serendipity in the paper-filled stacks, they counter with the simple convenience of electronic resources (Tewell, 2015). Against the inherent majesty of print collections, they place a mobile device that contains entire collections of books. As shown in figure 2.2, there has been a relentless shift in spending away from traditional formats to electronic information resources. This data, reported by the Publishers Communication Group (2016), shows that the percentage of library materials spending on electronic resources rose from less than 30 percent in 2004 to over 70 percent in 2015. The trend appears clear, and there is no reason to believe it will reverse itself in the foreseeable future.

Print and Digital Sources

As with many ongoing controversies, the debate over print versus electronic resources inevitably runs itself down to a single conclusion—the best course is neither print nor digital, but print *and* digital. A reference collection must be developed using good judgment and valid information to identify the best resources for the purpose at hand. The sticking point, of course, is the tricky term "best resources." What is best? Who decides, and how? In some ways, it is reminiscent of the old aphorism: when your only tool is a hammer, every task starts looking like a nail. For some who are untutored in library and research skills, the right tool is always Google or Wikipedia, regardless of the task. Librarians, too, have favorite resources, and are often reluctant to move outside of their comfort zones. It is the librarian, though, who must be endlessly vigilant regarding new and useful resources

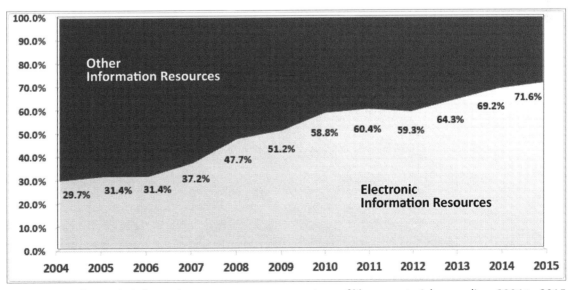

Figure 2.2. Electronic information resources as a percentage of library materials spending, 2004 to 2015

to accomplish research tasks more thoroughly and efficiently. This is exactly what patrons need—and have a right to expect—from their librarians. Admittedly, decisions concerning library resources can be difficult and fraught with controversy, but some of the following pieces of advice may help in making rational choices:

- *Objective statistics.* The best way to make collection development decisions is to use the most reliable, valid data available. Your library may or may not have the ability to undertake a major research project to determine the research needs of your patrons, but use any good information at your disposal. If possible, you should track the use of reference materials. You can normally obtain usage information from vendors for your electronic resources. For print resources in a non-circulating reference collection, you may have to track reshelving of reference books to determine usage. This is a labor-intensive process, but provides immense value in making decisions when purchasing new materials, or weeding old ones. Beyond simple usage, it may also be wise to perform a cost-per-use analysis of your collection. In an era of limited library funding, such data is helpful not only in making decisions about your collection, but also in defending those decisions to library patrons and administrators.
- *Differences by subject.* Another important criterion in making print/electronic decisions is the subject covered by the resource. Researchers in some disciplines tend to prefer more traditional formats, such as those studying history, literature, and other humanities. Disciplines such as business and medicine might lean toward electronic media. Naturally, there are exceptions to every rule, and any assumptions about the preferences of any group of patrons should be tested and communicated clearly before making sweeping changes.
- *Strategic collection development.* In some cases, decisions concerning the format of library resources may be connected to strategic objectives for collection development. A library may, for instance, decide to focus on materials related to job creation in the community, or the development of science and technology resources on a college campus. In other cases, agencies outside the library may provide funding to encourage these efforts. In such situations, it is often possible to add more advanced electronic resources for high-priority subjects, while other subject areas will focus on lower-cost, traditional materials.
- *Let the patrons decide.* When making decisions about the resources you will add to your library's collection, it is best to rely first and foremost on a deep knowledge of the needs of your patrons. This can be done through patron surveys and usage studies, but you should not underestimate the power of simply asking your patrons what they think. The answers may be varied and even self-contradictory, but with a bit of effort you should be able to obtain at least a rough idea of what your patrons will and will not use. Some libraries have moved to Patron Driven Acquisition (PDA), where almost all buying decisions are made by patrons.

The tips listed above may help to guide certain purchasing decisions for electronic reference materials, but difficult choices and conflicting opinions will always be a normal part of library collection development. There are few right or wrong answers, and there is usually more gray than black or white. With some tactful negotiation and a thoughtful approach to decisions, however, it is possible to keep your reference collection moving in a positive, productive direction. Nor is the format of library materials the only consideration in a modern collection. Discussed in the following subsections are a couple of examples of the many resources libraries can use to improve the quality, depth, and convenience of the reference services they provide.

Discovery Systems

Decades ago, old library card catalogs were retired to make way for online catalogs, and since then the procedure for searching for books and other library materials has been fairly consistent. Over time, the online catalog holdings were expanded to include records and links to various electronic books and journals, but the search process remained more or less the same. In recent years, however, a growing number of libraries have dropped the now-familiar online catalog in favor of discovery services—systems designed to search much more than the physical library collections. The exact services may vary by vendor but, in addition to searching through library holdings, discovery systems may allow full-text searches of electronic journals, journal aggregators, and even materials from online sources outside of the library. In short, these systems aim to be the closest thing libraries can offer to a Google-like one-stop search experience, though none of the discovery services currently on the market can fulfill these lofty ambitions completely.

One problem is that the vendors of library journal aggregators and indexes often resist loading their data through discovery services, or submit data in conflicting ways. In part, this may be because some vendors believe discovery systems are competing with their own indexes and abstracts, with the possibility of reduced demand for their products and services. For this reason, most discovery systems cannot truly provide results for *all* the library's materials. This situation is likely to ease as vendors realize that inclusion of their materials in library discovery systems will result in more users accessing and downloading materials from the vendors' products, leading to higher usage statistics and stronger customer demand (Breeding, 2014; Thompson, 2014).

Another major hurdle for discovery systems is the natural discomfort that users (including librarians) experience when dealing with a new system that approaches some tasks differently than traditional online catalogs did. Many library users are accustomed, for example, to finding encyclopedias listed in the library catalog, then either going to the physical volumes in the stacks or connecting to the online version through the vendor's website. A discovery system may, alternatively, automatically identify the encyclopedia entries and link to them directly within the discovery search results. Many people find this kind of thing disconcerting, though it is ultimately a useful function and a potential selling point.

Many normal functions are, in fact, handled differently in discovery systems. As another example, search results include individual articles pulled from journals and aggregators and link directly from the results list. Results may also include materials from outside the library altogether, such as Project Gutenberg, HathiTrust, and Wikipedia. With all these new additions to searches, the sheer volume of results can be overwhelming, and learning to understand the system may require time and patience. Despite these and several other growing pains, discovery services are likely to grow in prevalence and popularity as users become comfortable with the complex functionality, but enormous potential, of these new systems.

Finding Low-Cost, Useful Reference Sources on the Open Web

Reference collections cost money. They grow more expensive with each passing year as the demand for more detailed data and information rises and the cost of those resources skyrockets. At this time, there appears to be little chance that this trend will reverse itself, or even taper off. One small glimmer of hope, however, may be found in valuable research materials available for free on the open web. This is not to imply that expensive library resources are going away. Carefully reviewed and selected, though, free online resources can help fill out the reference collection and close gaps for specific subjects.

Free resources online are so numerous and varied that simply identifying a list of quality sites for any subject is a major undertaking and beyond the scope of this book. The list below is meant as a general overview of some broad areas you might consider in your search for free reference sources:

- *General sources.* A quick search of the Internet will yield numerous useful sources like Google Scholar, the Digital Library of America, and even the oft-maligned Wikipedia—which, as Zlatos (2012) argues so passionately, does indeed have a useful role to play in library reference services. Most librarians find, in fact, that their task is not so much gathering all useful resources on the Internet, but singling out the best of those resources for their patrons.

- *Government agencies and sites.* Governments spend enormous amounts of time and money gathering and archiving information. Fortunately, most of them will distribute at least a portion of their data to the public for free. Helpful international organizations include the World Health Organization, the United Nations, the International Monetary Fund, and the World Bank, all offering useful statistics and reports, many free or for a nominal fee. Federal agencies in the United States offer a wealth of information and resources, led by such valuable sources as American Factfinder, CIA World Factbook, and the National Oceanic and Atmospheric Administration. Many cities, states, and counties also provide free information that is invaluable to researchers.

- *Organizations and associations.* There are numerous groups and organizations that provide useful data, statistics, and general information online. This may range from trade associations like the International Coffee Organization, to educational groups like the American Federation of Teachers, to library organizations like the American Library Association or the Special Libraries Association. Resources on these sites may be free, but in some cases only association members can view them. One quite useful and publicly available offering is the Reference and User Services Association's "Best Free Reference Websites" list, which the organization has been making available on the RUSA site for almost 20 years.

- *Academic and library sources.* It should come as no surprise that colleges, universities, and libraries provide free access to all manner of research materials. Libraries aggressively pursue ways to provide free access, as exemplified in the University of California–Berkeley's "Freely Available Resources for Research," or Harvard University's "Free Legal Research Resources" (both can be located through a quick search on Google). Colleges and universities try to provide as much free access as possible through institutional repositories and faculty submissions to open access journals, many of which are available in searchable form in the Directory of Open Access Journals (DOAJ). This is not to mention the countless resources linked from the websites of university departments and individual faculty members.

The suggestions above are only a few examples among the countless sources available online. A word of caution is in order, however—it almost goes without saying that you must use your best judgment and perform due diligence on all web sources before advising them or linking them for your patrons. Ensure that each site is legitimate, maintained properly, and has been created by a trusted source.

⊚ Creating Research Guides and Tutorials

This may seem a strange place to find a discussion of library guides and tutorials, tucked down here after a section about electronic resources for reference services. There is little doubt, however, that in the current library environment, research guides and tutorials are created primarily for online access. There has been a movement in recent years to reach patrons where they live, and at this time many library patrons live online. While this is particularly true of millennials, people from every age group spend an increasing number of hours online, performing an expanding range of tasks and activities. It is vitally important, then, that libraries reach out to their patrons through the most effective media and formats available, and the profession is fortunate to have so many easy-to-use, readily accessible tools to help reach so many people in so many places.

In most libraries, moreover, it is the reference librarians who are called on to create research guides and tutorials. Jackson and Stacy-Bates (2016) report that all librarians responding to a recent survey confirmed that they were expected to create and maintain research guides and tutorials as a part of their jobs, while over 50 percent report that these responsibilities play a role in their evaluations. This same study uncovered another interesting reaction from its librarian respondents—when asked if they believed that creating and maintaining guides was worth the effort required, 66 percent responded affirmatively. The remaining librarians answered "maybe" or "it depends." The authors report that some respondents expanded on their answers by noting that patrons may have difficulty finding research guides on the library sites, and some even suggested that the quality of these guides was often lacking. It seems, overall, that librarians recognize the need to create guides, acknowledge their responsibility for taking this task upon themselves, and understand the difficulty of creating high-quality materials that are easily accessible for their patrons. While a detailed description of the fine points of creation and access to research guides is beyond the charge of this book, there are many excellent works on the subject, such as Rempel and Slebodnik's *Creating Online Tutorials* (2015), also in the Practical Guide for Librarians series. In the context of the current discussion of reference services, however, a brief overview of general form and strategies should set things moving in the right direction.

Decisions Concerning Content and Format

The subject and content of a guide are the first decisions you need to make. If the subject is not of interest to your users, or if the content of the guide does not cover the subject in a useful way, the guide will have little value to anyone. It is therefore imperative that you spend the time required to get to know your patrons well, whether they are university students at an academic library, community users at a public library, or account executives at a corporate library. You must develop a detailed understanding of their interests and work hard to remove the obstacles they face in finding the information they need. Build your guides around the questions your patrons ask, and add to your understanding by asking them follow-up questions. Always try to incorporate their suggestions into your work. This simple methodology should go a long way toward keeping your guides relevant to the needs of your patrons.

Once you have determined the subject of your guide, you will need to decide whether there are materials already available that you wish to provide to your patrons, or whether you will need to create your own materials. Some librarians have a strong preference for creating their own guides and tutorials, while others wish to avoid "reinventing the wheel" by re-creating content that already exists. A part of the decision may come down to personal preference, but ideally the deciding factor should be the effectiveness of the materials for the specific needs of your patrons. If you do decide to use existing guides created by other librarians, whether from your own library or from other libraries, always ask permission of the creators before using their work. Once you have received permission, you can simply create a link to an existing guide, or adapt the content for inclusion in your own guide. Remember, though, to give the original creators full credit for their work.

There are any number of other decisions to be made (and often changed and revised) throughout the process of developing library guides. For example, you must determine whether it is best to create a traditional guide made up primarily of text and images, a video tutorial, or some other format. In a usability study at St. John's University, Turner, Fuchs, and Todman (2015) found that freshmen completed library tasks more quickly and effectively after exposure to text-and-image tutorials than was the case after watching video tutorials. While interesting, this result should not be regarded as a universal endorsement of static guides over other formats. Many library users prefer video tutorials, and some dynamic processes (such as using a complicated scanner or touring library facilities) may be easier to describe using the video format. Other specific circumstances may call for the use of an audio podcast, a simple document, or PowerPoint slides. Remember, too, that there are circumstances in which asynchronous resources like guides and tutorials will not work nearly as well as providing real-time contact with a librarian. In these instances, the give-and-take of a phone conversation, or even an instant chat session, provides the necessary element of interaction—in this way participants can clear up misunderstandings or ask follow-up questions. Whatever the situation, remember that the best format is always the one that works best for your patrons, not the one that is easiest or least expensive for the library.

Tools

When you have decided what kind of library guides you would like to produce, you will need to choose the appropriate tools to create them. The good news is that there is an almost endless pool of software programs and applications to choose from. The bad news is that you may have to dive deep into that pool to find what you need, and this can be daunting. If possible, keep up with journals, blogs, and news sources offering reviews of the latest tools for librarians. You can also ask for suggestions from colleagues and acquaintances, or post questions to library-related forums. As a starting point, the items below describe some of the key tools you might use to create and distribute library guides and tutorials:

- *Content management systems.* These are applications that allow you to create web content without using HTML or other forms of coding. Once you have installed the system and set it up properly, it is relatively easy to create web pages. For some years, the most popular system has been Springshare's LibGuides. LibGuides is designed specifically for library use, and offers a number of add-ons covering such functions as a knowledge base, statistics, and event calendars. There is a fee for Lib-Guides, but it is low in comparison to many commercial systems, while providing solid functionality and a helpful support service. Other open source systems are available free of charge, but may require considerable back-end setup to fulfill the needs of a library. Among the most popular at this time are WordPress, Joomla, and Drupal, though new entrants appear on a regular basis.

- *Software for images and videos.* There are a number of applications available to help with the creation of images for library guides. Adobe's Photoshop and Illustrator are the big names in the field, though they do have a steep learning curve with a price tag to match. Microsoft's Publisher and Paint applications will suffice for most library needs, though if they are unavailable, an online search will reveal several free applications that can perform the essential functions. One specific task librarians rely on heavily is the screenshot—a snapshot of anything appearing on a computer screen. Greenshot is an excellent freeware version you can download to your computer, while Awesome Screenshot is just one of several good browser-based applications. For creating screen-capture videos, Jing is the perennial favorite among free versions, while Adobe's Captivate and Techsmith's Camtasia both carry a substantial fee but offer many useful bells and whistles.

- *Providing access.* Ensuring that your patrons can find and easily access your library's guides and tutorials is every bit as challenging as creating the materials in the first place. In addition to posting them to your library's website, video tutorials are often posted to YouTube and linked to other online sources as appropriate. Links to all your guides can be provided to patrons through various social media, blogs, course management systems (for students), professional and trade association pages and, if the guides are generalizable, even the web pages of other libraries.

General Tips and Advice

Tutorials and guides come in many varieties, and there are many ways to arrive at a successful result. Using a bit of creativity can provide a fresher, more interesting product, and there is always room to try a new and innovative approach. Experience indicates, however, that at least a few basic guidelines are worth incorporating into your efforts:

- *Focus on the basics.* Include only what is useful and necessary. Do not clutter your guide by trying to include everything. Most librarians find that organizing resources by importance is more helpful than organizing alphabetically. You can use headings and bullets to help to organize materials in an understandable way. Avoid scrolling where you can, and avoid the use of sub-tabs, as many users find them confusing or don't notice them at all.

- *Be clear.* Use a straightforward, conversational writing style, composed at a level appropriate for your readers. You should attempt to keep text passages brief and to the point, eliminating jargon and unnecessary technical terms where possible. Complex tasks can be broken down into small, understandable steps. It is also very important to name your guides in a way that gives clear indication of the content, using terms your users will understand.

- *Maintain your guides.* It can be very difficult to find the time to review your guides for mistakes and updates, but it is crucial to do so on a regular basis. Dead links are particularly troublesome. Many content management systems allow system-wide automatic link checking, but if your system lacks this convenience, you should still take the time to check links manually. Ultimately, proper maintenance of guides may mean limiting the number of guides you create to ensure that you can properly care for the ones you do have.

Key Points

This chapter has provided a general overview of what a reference collection means, how one is established, and what is involved in making decisions regarding the purchase of materials.

- The negative (and sometimes damaging) stereotype of the "know-it-all" librarian, despite its regular presence in books and films, has little resemblance to actual reference services providers, and should be opposed by those in the profession at every opportunity.
- A reference collection is anything that proves useful to staff and patrons as they pursue research projects and answer questions. Considerations regarding whether to purchase print or electronic versions of potential reference titles are many, and require a significant effort. In the end, however, the format matters far less than the content.
- Electronic reference sources are now a permanent part of reference work; the question is which ones to use, and how to make them available. Quality reference sources online do exist, and the technology for incorporating some of them with a search of library-specific holdings exists as well.
- Effective research guides and tutorials can enhance and highlight reference collections, but it's important to make them accessible and relevant to your library's core patron group.

The next chapter focuses on the people part of reference services, rather than on the collections: how to conduct an effective reference interview, and how to use the available reference technology to your advantage.

Note

1. A modified version of the rest of this subsection was previously published in Katherine Pennavaria's book, *Genealogy: A Practical Guide for Librarians* (Rowman & Littlefield, 2015).

References

Ashhurst, John. 1901. "On Taking Ourselves Too Seriously." *Library Journal* 26, no. 5 (May): 265–68.

Bailey, Bill. 1987. "The '55 Percent Rule' Revisited." *Journal of Academic Librarianship* 13, no. 5 (November): 280–82.

Boswell, John. 1791. *The Life of Samuel Johnson.* Accessed via Project Gutenberg, http://www.gutenberg.org/files/1564/1564-h/1564-h.htm.

Breeding, Marshall. 2014. "Web-Scale Discovery Services: Finding the Right Balance." *American Libraries* 45, no. 1/2 (January–February): 25.

Burns, Grant. 1998. *Librarians in Fiction: A Critical Bibliography*. Jefferson, NC: McFarland & Co.

Cordell, Rosanne. 2014. "Optimizing Library Services: Managing the 21st-Century Reference Collection." *Against the Grain* 26, no. 4 (September): 53–54.

Durrance, Joan C. 1989. "Reference Success: Does the 55 Percent Rule Tell the Whole Story?" *Library Journal* 114, no. 7 (April 15): 31–36.

Eco, Umberto. 1983. *The Name of the Rose*. San Diego: Harcourt Brace Jovanovich.

Evans, G. Edward, and Thomas L. Carter. 2009. *Introduction to Library Public Services*. 7th ed. Westport, CT: Libraries Unlimited.

Freed, Ben. 2015. "University of Michigan Unveils State of the Art Medical Library." Retrieved from MLive.com, http://www.mlive.com/news/ann-arbor/index.ssf/2015/08/university_of _michigan_unveils_2.html.

Hernon, Peter, and Charles R. McClure. 1986. "Unobtrusive Reference Testing: The 55 Percent Rule." *Library Journal* 111, no. 7 (April 15): 37–41.

Howe, Harriet E. 1936. "Traits of the Ideal and the Potential Librarian." *Library Quarterly* 6.2 (Apr): 111–23.

Hubbertz, Andrew. 2007. "The Fallacy in the 55 Percent Rule." *Documents to the People* 35, no. 3 (Fall): 15–17.

"The Ideal Librarian." 1882. *Library Journal* 7, no. 6 (June): 106.

Jackson, Rebecca, and Kristine K. Stacy-Bates. 2016. "The Enduring Landscape of Online Subject Research Guides." *Reference and User Services Quarterly* 55, no. 3 (Spring): 219–29.

Jardine, Carolyn. 1995. "Maybe the 55 Percent Rule Doesn't Tell the Whole Story: A User-Satisfaction Survey." *College and Research Libraries* 56, no. 6 (November): 477–85.

Ji, Sung Wook, Sherri Michaels, and David Waterman. 2014. "Print vs. Electronic Readings in College Courses: Cost-Efficiency and Perceived Learning." *Internet and Higher Education* 21 (April): 17–24.

Katz, William A. 1998. *Cuneiform to Computer: A History of Reference Sources*. Lanham, MD: Scarecrow.

Kroeger, Alice Bertha. 1902. *Guide to the Study and Use of Reference Books: A Manual for Librarians, Teachers and Students*. Chicago: American Library Association.

Lederer, Naomi. 2016. "Why Libraries Should Retain a Core Print Reference Collection." *The Reference Librarian* 57, no. 4 (October–December): 307–22.

Lopatovska, Irene, and Deanna Sessions. 2016. "Understanding Academic Reading in the Context of Information-Seeking." *Library Review* 65, no. 8/9: 502–18.

Massis, Bruce E. 2011. "'Serendipitous' Browsing Versus Library Space." *New Library World* 112, no. 3/4: 178–82.

Mizrachi, Diane. 2015. "Undergraduates' Academic Reading Format Preferences and Behaviors." *Journal of Academic Librarianship* 41, no. 3: 301–11.

Posner, Beth. 2002. "Know-It-All Librarians." *Reference Librarian* 37, no. 78: 111–19. http://aca demicworks.cuny.edu/cgi/viewcontent.cgi?article=1020&context=gc_pubs.

Publishers Communication Group. 2016. "Library Budget Predications for 2016 (White Paper)." Boston: Publishers Communication Group. http://www.pcgplus.com/white-papers/.

Rempel, Hannah Gascho, and Maribeth Slebodnik. 2015. *Creating Online Tutorials: A Practical Guide for Librarians*. Lanham, MD: Rowman & Littlefield.

Richardson, Ernest Cushing. 1896. "Reference Books." In *Papers Prepared for the World's Library Congress, Held at the Columbian Exposition*, edited by Melvil Dewey, 976–82. Washington, DC: Government Printing Office.

Riley, Sharon. 2014. "Academic: New Florida University Unveils Bookless Library." *Library Journal* 139, no. 15: 13.

Singer, Carol A. 2010. "Ready Reference Collections: A History." *Reference & User Services Quarterly* 49, no. 3 (Spring): 253–64.

Skipton, Michael D., and Jeannie Bail. 2014. "Cognitive Processes and Information Literacy: Some Initial Results from a Survey of Business Students' Learning Activities." *Journal of Business and Finance Librarianship* 19, no. 3: 181–233.

Smith, Lloyd. 1876. "The Qualifications of a Librarian." *American Library Journal* 1, no. 2 (November 30): 69–74.

Terrell, Heather B. 2015. "Reference Is Dead, Long Live Reference: Electronic Collections in the Digital Age." *Information Technology and Libraries* 34, no. 4 (December): 55–62.

Tewell, Eamon C. 2015. "Multiple Factors Influence Undergraduates' Intent to Use Online Library Resources." *Evidence-Based Library & Information Practice* 10, no. 4: 235–37.

Thompson, JoLinda. 2014. *Implementing Web-Scale Discovery Services: A Practical Guide for Librarians.* Lanham, MD: Rowman & Littlefield.

Turner, Benjamin, Carolyn Fuchs, and Anthony Todman. 2015. "Static vs. Dynamic Tutorials: Applying Usability Principles to Evaluate Online Point-of-Need Instruction." *Information Technology & Libraries* 3, no. 4 (December): 30–54.

Tyckoson, David A. 2011. "Issues and Trends in the Management of Reference Services: A Historical Perspective." *Journal of Library Administration* 51, no. 3: 259–78.

Woolf, Virginia. 1932. "Dr. Burney's Evening Party." *The Common Reader, Second Series.* London: Hogarth Press and New York: Harcourt, Brace & World.

Zlatos, Christy. 2012. "It's Free, It's Interactive, and It's Available to All: Embracing Wikipedia at the Reference Desk and Beyond." In *Leading the Reference Renaissance: Today's Ideas for Tomorrow's Cutting-Edge Services*, edited by Marie L. Radford, 333–46. New York: Neal-Schuman.

CHAPTER 3

Putting Reference Services into Practice

IN THIS CHAPTER

▷ Conducting the reference interview effectively

▷ Using virtual reference technology

▷ Identifying trends in reference services

WITH ALL THE ACTIVITIES TAKING PLACE at libraries today, some patrons might be unaware that there is such a thing as a reference desk, and that the library has employees dedicated to answering questions. Public libraries host book clubs, holiday-themed parties, and even yoga classes. Their conference room spaces can be found occupied by tax advisors and tutors, and the employees may, at any time, be dressed in costume as part of a sponsored activity. College libraries have their quiet spaces and vault-like stacks, but the common areas and spaces set aside for student activities usually hum with action.

Much of this busy-ness at libraries takes place around, but not in connection with, the reference desk, which at most libraries is in a visible and central place (though never as close to the front entrance as the circulation desk, if those two entities are separated). Only when the library user needs help—pursuing a research project, finding something in the library stacks, getting a question answered—does he or she approach the desk. Users of the library's web pages operate similarly—they browse, use the catalog, and explore linked pages, but acknowledge the reference desk by phone, email, or chat window only when they realize they need help.

So, a reference service is quintessentially need-based; reference services simply would not exist if people did not have questions. As discussed in chapter 1, those questions have changed over the decades as information technology has gone light-years beyond the telephone, typewriter, and printed book. The role of the reference services provider has changed substantially as well, as questions have become more complex and resources have multiplied like enthusiastically procreating small mammals. As a result of these changes, the reference interview—always the heart of a reference interaction—has become both more important and more difficult to get right. Library patrons come in with an incredible variety of questions, many of them unpredictable and difficult to answer. The digital resources and tools now in the hands of library employees would take multiple lifetimes to master—how does the reference services practitioner offer efficient and effective service with so many options? That is the question explored in this chapter.

The Reference Interview

As a rule, library users do not clearly and concisely state their information needs to reference services staff. A college student seeking a map showing the topography of the ancient Middle East might approach the desk and ask, "Do you guys have any maps?" A public library user looking for a do-it-yourself manual on how to install a garage-door system might ask, "Where's your books on electrical stuff?" We've all been there.

Often library users are unsure whether they are asking the right person and how to phrase their questions, or they might be unclear on what exactly they need. In general, reference services providers can assume that those who approach the desk, send an email, make a phone call, or initiate a chat window have some idea of what they want, but might need some help communicating the specifics. That's why the *reference interview* is so important: as the contact point between seeker and provider of information, this interaction carries the burden of whether the library user goes away satisfied or dissatisfied with the service. All else about the library—its location, furnishings, print and online collections, size—matters less than its staff and the interactions patrons have with them.

When someone has an unsatisfactory interaction with one employee of a library, later on that someone might say, "Those people at the library aren't very nice," or even "Library people are never helpful." One unhelpful staff member can stand, in a patron's mind, for the entire crew. It's an unfair reality, but one that should be addressed in staff training. Each library employee needs to be told at least once that he or she represents the library when any interaction occurs between staff and patron. In other words, it's not Amanda or Jason who is answering the question, but *the library*. Because the association between library staff and the library itself is so strong in the minds of users, getting the reference interview right matters quite a bit. And getting it right involves knowing something about the interpersonal dynamics of that interaction, and committing yourself to improving.

Many articles and books have been written about the nature and importance of the library reference interview. One well-received recent publication is Dave Harmeyer's *The Reference Interview Today: Negotiating and Answering Questions Face to Face, On the Phone, and Virtually* (2014). Harmeyer, a professor and administrator at Azusa Pacific University, takes an optimistic, energetic view of the reference interview in today's libraries. After a thorough review of the research literature on reference interviews, he sketches out 13 scenarios, each illustrating some principle of the reference interview ideal. After each scenario, he asks questions that help the reader analyze the encounter between patron and library staff. Harmeyer steers readers to his blog (https://referenceinterview.wordpress.com/author/dharmeyer) for the purpose of "continuing the conversation" (2014: 10), but at the time this chapter was written (December 2016), only one entry has appeared—a description of the blog's purpose.

Harmeyer is far from the only information science scholar interested in the reference interview. The *Library Literature & Information Science Full Text (H.W. Wilson)* database, available via EBSCOhost, lists 180 articles published between 1984 and 2015 that have the phrase "reference interview" somewhere in the record; in 140 of those, the phrase appears in the title of the article. Few other library-related subjects are discussed as thoroughly as the reference interview.

In 1996, the Reference and User Services Association (RUSA), a division of the American Library Association, published its first set of guidelines for reference interviews. Those guidelines include the following areas of relevance:

- *Approachability.* In general, seek to make the patron "feel comfortable in a situation which may be perceived as intimidating, risky, confusing, and overwhelming." More specifically, be "poised and ready to engage," and establish a connection with eye contact, a smile, and a friendly greeting.
- *Interest.* Exhibit a "high level of interest" in each inquiry by facing the patron, maintaining eye contact, and appearing focused and unhurried.
- *Listening/inquiring.* Communicate effectively, first by speaking in a "cordial and encouraging manner"; second, by rephrasing the request and asking open-ended questions; and third, by avoiding jargon and clarifying terminology. Finally, it should go without saying (but RUSA says it anyway) that the reference services provider should not voice value judgments about the subject matter of the inquiry.
- *Searching.* Learn to search effectively for whichever context you work in (e.g., public, academic, law, or children's library), but also to involve the patron in the search by requesting confirmation as it proceeds and explaining the search process itself. And learn to recognize when it is appropriate to refer a patron to another library or resource.
- *Follow-up.* Ask if the patron's question has been answered satisfactorily and invite the person to return to the reference desk later with further needs. If you are referring someone to another librarian or resource, make a print-out or write the directions/phone number on a slip of paper.

For that final step in the process, readers might find useful a phrase borrowed from the world of retail booksellers: some managers instruct bookstore employees to put a book in the customer's hand after a person asks a question. For example, someone asks, "Where are your cookbooks?" The bookstore employee could simply point to the appropriate aisle, but a better (and more profitable) way is to take the customer to the cookbook section and ask for specifics on what the person is looking for, or point out some popular titles—in both cases, the key to better sales is to pull a book off the shelf and hand it to the customer. That simple gesture results in more sales, but also makes the customers feel they have received good service.

A reference services provider should take the managers' advice literally—give each patron something to take away, whether it's a printout, a slip of paper with call numbers, or a suggestion form. In other words, avoid letting patrons walk away with nothing to show from their contact with a library staffer. "No, I'm sorry, we don't have that" is not good enough; instead, offer the person something similar, or look the title up in another library's catalog, or explain the interlibrary loan process. Tell them you'll put in a request for the item to be added to the library's collections, or give them the name and number of a local expert who may be able to suggest other resources. Librarians who practice the "put a book in the customer's hand" philosophy don't necessarily drive up sales, but they will increase the sales counterpart: patron satisfaction, and rate of return to the service point.

Figure 3.1 neatly expresses a generalized four-step process for completing a successful reference interview. As the chart indicates, the reference services provider will get better results by asking "open" questions, even in the greeting. For example, say "What can I help you with today?" rather than "Can I help you?"—the latter can only be answered with a YES or NO, and communication has not progressed at all. It's a silly question anyway, because obviously the answer is YES—otherwise the person would not be contacting the library. Anyone who staffs a desk should stop asking this meaningless question and replace it with a more open, inviting one.

Understanding the Question

Reference services providers can and should alter behavior and modify words to achieve the goal of an effective interaction. At the core of the reference interaction, however, is the key issue of understanding what is being asked. As already established, many inquirers at libraries do not phrase their questions precisely, but are likely to generalize their need, asking for "books about animals" rather than a source that explains how to teach obedience to a puppy. Patrons simply might not know whether their information needs can be met in that location and with available resources. Thus, figuring out exactly what someone wants is the most important job of the reference services provider.

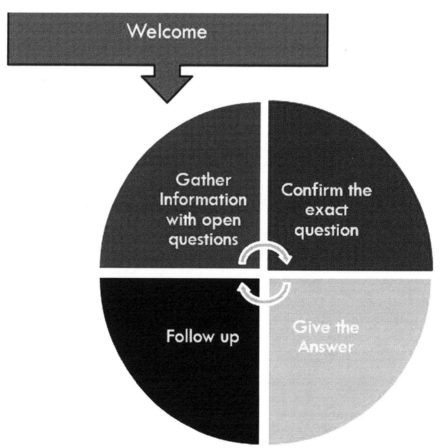

Figure 3.1.   The reference interview process. https://www.haikudeck.com/reference-services-education-presentation-9UAUzBGIEh. *Source:* Chart created by Emily Mann, Florida State University

Many readers of this book will be familiar with the 1989 self-help publication, *The 7 Habits of Highly Effective People*, by Stephen R. Covey. Among the "powerful lessons in personal change" that Covey recommends is Habit #4: "Seek first to understand, then to be understood." The wisdom of this advice is undeniable, and especially relevant to public service librarians. People enter, text, email, and call libraries with questions, and effective reference service depends on understanding and acting on those questions. Conducting a successful reference interview means, among other things, being a good listener. People who provide answers for a living, sometimes in a busy environment, want to deal with questions quickly and efficiently, and do what they do best: connect seekers of information with the information they seek. Quite often, such as when the library is busy, they have no choice but to throw out the answers quickly and move on to the next inquirer.

The elements of being a good listener are well established and can all be applied to reference services. According to the crowd-sourced repository of collective wisdom called WikiHow (2015), there are three facets to good listening:

- *Listen with an open mind.* University library reference desk personnel do not regularly field questions from non-affiliated users, and public library staffers do not generally deal with university students. But such encounters could and do happen. Listening with an open mind means not presuming you already know the context from which a person speaks, or the level of expertise that person already possesses.
- *Know what to say.* What you say first, of course, sets the tone for the interaction. Your greeting matters. You can always glance up and say, "Yes?" but is that really the best greeting? Even "Can I help you?" is a poor choice. Say instead, "What can I help you with?" or "How can I help you?" Then consider what to say after someone has asked a question. Asking for clarification is appropriate. Knowing what to say also involves knowing what *not* to say. No one wants to hear, "We've been getting that question *all day*."
- *Use appropriate body language.* Eye contact and a smile are appropriate—a frown and quick glance before looking away are not.

That third element of being a good listener bears further expansion. Everyone gives off signals with body language, but it's harder to perceive non-verbal signals than it is to hear our own words. Decades ago, a successful speaker on leadership methods and customer service skills named Arch Lustberg created a video presentation tailored to library personnel. Called "Controlling the Confrontation," Lustberg's (1989) video aimed at giving library staff and administrators some practical advice for dealing with hostile patrons and news reporters. Though initially aimed at library staff, his advice works well for anyone dealing with a difficult personal encounter. In general, he advises someone thus confronted to de-escalate the situation by using simple, unemotional language and by avoiding using the language of the confronter (e.g., "You called me stupid"—"I did NOT call you stupid").

But his most important advice has to do with the nonverbal part of the response: "Open your face," he says, "by raising your eyebrows." To get the effect Lustberg means, think of how your face (usually) looks when you see a baby. You not only smile, but your eyebrows go up involuntarily, especially if there's a chance you can get a smile back from the baby.

Using audience volunteers, Lustberg demonstrates in the video that a concentrated effort to keep the eyebrows slightly elevated results in a more "open" expression and even a more genuine and believable smile. He even asks his volunteers to say negative things while maintaining that raised-eyebrow/smiling face, and most of them cannot do so convincingly. Of course, it's possible to smile without lifting the eyebrows, he points out, but if you remember that one small movement, you will not only improve your smile but will actually alter your tone of voice. He repeats this point: an open face will help any interaction, *even when that interaction is not face-to-face*. Simply put, the open face alters the paralanguage of the interaction: your expression and the tone in your voice. With these things altered, he says, your words will also change for the better.

Arch Lustberg's advice helped a generation of librarians deal with difficult patrons and situations. His video, sadly, never made it to DVD, and copies of it now exist only in deteriorating VHS tapes. He gave other presentations, of course, and some of them are still available and contain his excellent advice. Lustberg, who died in early 2015, often closed his presentations with a quotation relevant to the reference services provider: "Tell me and I'll forget. Show me, and I'll remember. Involve me, and I'll understand." Though this aphorism's origins are disputed, its wisdom cannot be.

Emotional Intelligence

Interacting with other people successfully requires thought and consideration. But in what direction should someone focus those thoughts? One way to view social interactions is through the lens of *emotional intelligence*, a concept developed in the early 1980s and still discussed in reference to libraries.

According to *A Dictionary of Psychology* (Coleman, 2008), emotional intelligence (EI) is the ability to understand emotions, one's own and that of others—to label them accurately and respond to them appropriately. The concept, though not the term, was introduced by Howard Gardner, a well-known developmental psychologist, in his 1983 publication, *Frames of Mind: Theories of Multiple Intelligences*. The initial use of the term "emotional intelligence" has not been definitively established, but it began to appear in research literature about psychology shortly after Gardner's book was published. In 1995, another book, Daniel Goleman's *Emotional Intelligence*, brought the term into popular use.

Goleman's book spent over a year on the *New York Times* non-fiction best-seller list, and he quickly produced another book for the now-hot market on EI. The second book, *Working with Emotional Intelligence* (1998), focused on workplace applications of the theory, and is perhaps the more relevant for the working librarian. Goleman notes that customers (read: library patrons) come seeking knowledge and information, but they also are looking for interpersonal qualities such as empathy, which is part of emotional intelligence. To develop your EI, says Goleman, you must focus on two related "competencies": personal and social. *Personal* competency is about managing yourself; *social* is about handling relationships with others. Conducting an effective reference interview and providing quality reference services involves paying attention to both.

Personal competencies, according to Goleman, involves three facets: self-awareness, self-regulation, and motivation. *Self-awareness* is simply knowing yourself—knowing what environment you prefer to work in, knowing the sights and sounds that please or displease you, and above all, knowing how you learn. One theory of learning styles is based on the same Jungian concepts that the popular Myers-Briggs personality assessment test derives from; another theory focuses on whether an individual is primarily a *visual*, *auditory*, or *kinesthetic* learner. Whichever theory is applied, the reference services provider seeking to improve his or her emotional intelligence will benefit from increasing self-awareness about learning styles.

The second facet of personal competency, *self-regulation*, involves managing your inner self—your impulses, thoughts, and decisions. An innate tendency to speak before thinking, as occurs with strongly extroverted people, can be controlled through conscious effort. Conversely, a lifelong habit of avoiding speaking to strangers must be overcome in the reference services environment. In other words, thoughts and impulses cannot be totally suppressed, but they can be regulated. The third facet, *motivation*, involves internal characteristics like initiative and optimism. As a reference services provider, you can communicate your motivation to succeed in the interaction by intentionally using a warm voice tone and "I'm approachable" body language.

But personal competencies are only part of the emotional intelligence equation. Perhaps even more important are social competencies, which are all about relationships with other people. Each interaction with another person, whether a fellow staffer or someone who approaches the reference desk, establishes or continues a relationship that can be examined and managed. Granted, the "relationship" might last only a few minutes, but it ends happily or unhappily, just as longer ones do. Reference services providers would improve their social competencies by learning to build successful relationships, even if most advice along that line is not aimed at the brief reference interview.

There are two "social competencies," according to Goleman: *empathy* and *social skills*. Empathy comes more easily to some people than others, but everyone can learn to recognize its presence or absence, and take steps to acquire it. Empathy derives from the Greek word *pathos*, "feeling." It doesn't involve our own feelings, but rather indicates an awareness of other peoples' feelings and the context from which they view the world. Empathy can be indicated by mirroring, which is the conscious or subconscious replication of another person's verbal and non-verbal signals. Mirroring does not mean aping another's behavior; if done consciously, it should be done so subtly that the other person never thinks about it. For example, a patron approaches the reference desk in an easy manner, with a smile and friendly tone of voice. Appropriate mirroring would reflect that easiness and warmth without calling attention to itself. However, if someone begins the reference interaction more formally, with a certain stiffness and correctness in tone, words, and posture, the best response is to sit up a bit straighter and speak in a courteous, interested way that could seem too impersonal by the person described in the first example. Mirroring makes others feel more comfortable, and makes us appear "normal" to them.

Empathy also involves paying attention to the learning style of the person asking a question. Some inquirers are happier receiving minimal information before being shown the way to the stacks; others prefer to see how the information was retrieved before they leave the desk. Enhancing your empathy skills will certainly improve your reference interactions. When someone does not respond appropriately, a jarring effect is created, and the likelihood of the "relationship" ending positively is diminished. Imagine someone who uses a wheelchair (but doesn't say so) emailing the reference desk: "I've noticed that the library elevator is frequently out of order. Is that problem being fixed?" Now imagine a grossly inappropriate response: "LOL! Just think about how much exercise you'll get taking the stairs." Yet this flippant response *would* be appropriate in a different context, like in response to a text message from a fellow staffer saying, "OMG the stupid elevator is out again!" In that case, a formal reply, the one appropriate for the wheelchair inquirer, would hit the wrong note. It's all about knowing and adjusting to the other person's context, perceptions, and feelings. Library patrons as a rule do not adjust themselves to us, so as reference services providers, we must assume that burden.

Dewdney and Michell suggested in 1996 that some library patrons ask questions merely to establish answers to bigger, but unspoken, ones, such as "Am I in the right place? Am I interrupting this person?" To deal with these unspoken questions, they advise reference desk staffers to remember the letters P.A.C.T. for every patron encounter. You want to send them the message, verbally or non-verbally, that they are in the right **P**lace, that you are **A**vailable, that they have made **C**ontact with the person who can help, and that their **T**opic has been heard. Everyone sends messages, whether they are consciously done or not, so why not intentionally send these helpful messages? By addressing the unspoken needs of the inquirer at the reference desk, you will exhibit good listening skills and set the stage for future reference interactions with that person.

The message of both Gardner's and Goleman's books is the same: human beings have a variety of "intelligences," of which the traditional IQ (Intelligence Quotient) test measures only a small slice. The truth of that concept seems fairly obvious now, but for many decades the only intelligence assumed to be worth measuring was that of reasoning and intellect. In social interactions, however, superior reasoning skills are a poor ally; more valuable socially is superior *emotional* or *social* intelligence—an ability to "read" people and respond appropriately. The librarian interested in creating a highly effective reference services environment would do well to study the work of Gardner and Goleman and incorporate their ideas into staff training. Responding appropriately to those who approach the reference desk involves more than knowing the answers to questions.

They make excellent reading, but Gardner and Goleman's books were aimed at a general audience, and were produced over 20 years ago. For library administrators and staff, a closer look at more recent applications of the emotional intelligence theory to reference services may be helpful.

Papers exploring the connection between emotional intelligence in the context of libraries, librarians, and information literacy are routinely published in the academic literature. In 2013, two such papers were presented at the Association for College and Research Libraries annual conference (and subsequently published in conference proceedings): "Emotional Intelligence and the Winds of Change in Academic Libraries" (Hendrix) and "Feeling Our Way: Emotional Intelligence and Information Literacy Competency" (Matteson, Farooq, and Mease).

According to Hendrix, the "winds of change" currently blowing through library systems have resulted partly from the repeated questioning, in the media and popular culture, of whether libraries as physical spaces have a future. How people perceive librarians and the jobs they do has shifted considerably over the years; libraries have undergone internal restructuring (including financial), which sometimes results in them being run more like businesses than not-for-profit entities. Indeed, even the nature of a university education has changed, along with how we all do research. All of this change has affected library users to some degree, but the people most affected are those who work in libraries, particularly in areas of public services such as the reference desk. Consequently, Hendrix sees value in applying emotional intelligence theory to staff training and development: helping those who work in this changing environment manage themselves better by giving them a way to perceive their own emotional intelligence and see how to enhance it. Improving "workplace emotion," she says, can make inevitable changes ordered by higher level administrators easier to adapt to and even embrace. And remember that someone with a low EI quotient can obstruct change, and prevent others from accepting it.

Other recent papers have explored EI theory scientifically, as a tool for enhancing library services. The 2012 International Conference on Innovation, Management, and Technology Research, held in Malaysia, included a presentation (and subsequent publication in proceedings) called "The Development of Librarian Emotional Intelligence Assessment Tool" (Masrek and Sani). Even the journal *Library Hi Tech News* has published articles about this relatively low-tech theory, such as "Emotional Intelligence in a Stupid World" (Klare, Behney, and Kenney, 2014), which recommends hiring people who display high levels of emotional intelligence, even for entry-level positions.

The first big question, of course, is how you test emotional intelligence, and the second is whether you can attain a higher level through effort. Several tools have been developed to address the first question. The University of New Hampshire maintains web pages devoted to the issue of emotional intelligence (http://www.unh.edu/emotional_intelligence); these pages are not the most sophisticated presentation of material (links are labeled "click here" rather than icons or words being made into hyperlinks), but it covers the general information on EI fairly well. The page set is described as "a site dedicated to communicating scientific information about emotional intelligence, including relevant aspects of emotions, cognition, and personality." Here you can find answers to the big questions of how EI is tested, and whether it can be enhanced or increased through effort.

The site was created by John D. Mayer, a University of New Hampshire psychologist who codeveloped the standard EI test, called the Mayer-Salovey-Caruso Emotional Intelligence Test (MSCEIT). The other primary creator, Peter Salovey, is, with Mayer, a leading authority on the theory of EI; Salovey is also the current president of Yale University. Mayer, the author of the web pages, describes the MSCEIT as an "ability" test—there are correct and incorrect answers to the questions. In other words, the evaluator does not rely on participants' own self-judgment relating to emotional intelligence; other tests allow for self-reporting. The MSCEIT is copyright-protected and available from Multi Health Systems (http://www.mhs.com).

A more concise source for a summary description of the MSCEIT is the page maintained by the Consortium for Research on Emotional Intelligence in Organizations (2015) (http://www.eiconsortium.org/measures/msceit.html). On the CREIO page, the four "branches" of emotional intelligence are described as:

- *Perceiving emotions.* The ability to perceive emotions in oneself and others, as well as in objects, art, stories, music, and other stimuli
- *Facilitating thought.* The ability to generate, use, and feel emotion as necessary to communicate feelings or employ them in other cognitive processes
- *Understanding emotions.* The ability to understand emotional information, to understand how emotions combine and progress through relationship transitions, and to appreciate such emotional meanings
- *Managing emotions.* The ability to be open to feelings, and to modulate them in oneself and others so as to promote personal understanding and growth

According to Jordan, Ashton-James, and Ashkanasy, this test has "the strongest theoretical and empirical support among the competing definitions of emotional intelligence" (2006: 190–91).

But other tests are available. The Emotional and Social Competence Inventory (ESCI), developed by Daniel Goleman and Richard Boyatzis, includes a "360-degree assessment," which consists of input gathered from those around the individual being tested (coworkers, family, friends). That input is compared to the self-reported data. According to McEnrue and Groves, the ECSI could be useful in identifying an individual who might serve as a "change catalyst" or who would exhibit "flexibility in handling change" (2006: 37). The Emotional and Social Competence Inventory is available through Hay Group (http://www.haygroup.com). Of course, several free versions of EI tests are available online.

So yes, emotional intelligence can be tested. Can it be improved? Mayer, at his University of New Hampshire site, says yes. But Mayer puts the emphasis on increasing emotional *knowledge*, which by its nature is a flexible quantity, capable of being added to or subtracted from a person's mind. Intelligence implies something innate and, perhaps, unchangeable. Knowledge, on the other hand, can always be gained through study and experience. At his site, in a section called "Improving Emotional Knowledge and Social Effectiveness, Mayer (2015) states,

> It may not matter, however, whether emotional intelligence can be raised or not. When most people ask the question, what they may mean is "Is it possible for someone to increase his or her emotional knowledge?" and, perhaps, "Is it possible for someone to improve their social and emotional functioning?" In both cases, the answer is almost certainly yes.

In other words, it's better to focus more on the role of knowledge instead of intelligence, and on the success of social/emotional functioning.

Library administrators who hire and supervise staff, and reference services providers who interact with patrons, could benefit by applying the theory of emotional intelligence to their decisions, and may want to take the standardized tests themselves. The value of making library employees aware of their own EI level, and of giving them ways to enhance their emotional knowledge, is demonstrable and fairly obvious. After all, as Goleman observes in *Working with Emotional Intelligence*, "out-of-control emotions can make smart people stupid" (1998: 22).

Modes of Communication

According to Courtney Selby in his 2007 article, "The Evolution of the Reference Interview," the tools and methods involved in the reference interview have changed over the years, but its basic purpose has not. The most common mode of interaction—face to face—was once the only mode available, and is still, says Selby, the "benchmark" for thinking about reference transactions, and the filter through which we see all other types. Telephone interactions are common now, but the approach is generally the same as in person.

The truly different interaction is online, when the "voice" of the speaker is masked by uniform type displayed onscreen, either via email or instant messaging (also known as *chat*). Libraries were early adopters of technology that allowed interaction via screen, says Selby. They started working with web-based chat room software in the early 1990s that allowed Internet Relay Chat (IRC)—essentially a forum with multiple channels on which users could "speak." But because each channel had (potentially) multiple users, the reference librarian could not really control the nature of the conversation on any particular channel, and sometimes users' questions went unanswered or were hijacked by other users. This "synchronous reference service" (because, like face-to-face and phone interactions, it happens in real time) had multiple problems and was, for the most part, eventually abandoned in favor of other types of contact.

Email, which developed even earlier than the IRC software, became popular as a method of interaction; though "asynchronous," it was preferred by librarians and users both as the best alternative to face-to-face or phone contact. One major advantage: users had time, as they wrote their email messages, to think about what they were asking, and consider the best phrasing to meet their needs. Or rather, they had the opportunity to take the time; many emailed requests received by reference desks are just as vague as those staffers hear in person (e.g., "Do you have any books about Africa?"). And emailed requests tend to take more time to address than real-time ones.

The problem of time-consuming requests is one concern that Naomi Lederer mentions in her 2001 article, "E-Mail Reference: Who, When, Where, and What Is Asked." She wonders whether asynchronous communication is too easily used by "non-affiliates"—people not connected to the library that offers the reference services. Other concerns have to do with the quality of the reference interview itself. During a synchronous exchange, says Lederer, an understanding of the user's information needs is more easily reached. Also, someone sending an email with a reference question might receive a reply quickly, but might not—and perhaps the "need to know" window has already closed. Finally, emailed questions and answers are vulnerable to unauthorized sharing; privacy concerns are relevant here in a way they are not during synchronous interaction.

The rise of instant messaging (i.e., chat) bridged the gap between synchronous forum channels and asynchronous emails—the communication is almost synchronous, but it still has the back-and-forth of email along with its relative privacy. Taken together, these digital forms of interaction are usually called "virtual" reference—a term not all library scholars agree accurately describes what is happening. "Digital" reference is sometimes used as an alternative; though they have different shadings of meaning, both terms indicate forms of interaction that take place via screen and do not involve face-to-face or phone contact. These digital conversations are especially popular with university students, but the service provider misses something vital when reading an on-screen query—the "visual and aural cues" that make up part of a face-to-face contact (Selby, 2007: 42). It's not easy to tell whether someone is confident or hesitant just by reading a message.

Personal contact not only helps to establish the user's needs easier, but also allows a subtext to be communicated by the library person through non-verbal signals ("I'm here. I'm friendly!") that digital contact does not allow. The librarian who answers an emailed question or an instant message with a few words does not really have a chance to establish a connection with the inquirer; the interaction is depersonalized in a way that concerns many who provide and write about reference services. Following up is also made more problematic—how can you know that the person walking by the desk today is the same one who emailed a question yesterday? One way to counteract the built-in depersonalized quality of email or chat interactions: use emoticons, the number of which grows, it seems, every day. Emoticons convey a gentle humor that makes the information provider seem like a real person rather than a thinking machine that can type.

In her 2003 article, "The Reference Interview Online," Jana Ronan summarizes her observations about the communication norms and conventions for online chat (she does not include email in the discussion), all of which are still relevant today. In general (i.e., not necessarily relating to library services), chat communication includes the following characteristics:

- Lack of non-verbal cues, voice intonation, and accent
- Language more like spoken than written
- Fluid identity and reduced inhibitions
- Use of emoticons
- Fast pace

Ronan also notes that chat initiators (and by extension, those who make contact via text or email) tend to use established abbreviations such as "K" for "OK" and "BTW" for "by the way" (2003: 43). As most people are already aware, use of all capital letters (TRY THIS LINK) can sound like you are shouting at your audience; generational differences in language use might also create problems. And users who contact the library via chat sometimes forget that it takes the person answering a question the same amount of time regardless of how contact is made; indeed, a chat contact could take longer than a face-to-face interaction because of all the missing non-verbal cues.

Even though email was already well established, and many institutions had already created HTML-based web pages that included the option to ask questions via online forms, the Reference and User Services Association did not specifically address the issue of virtual reference in its 1996 guidelines. But in 2003, RUSA established its "Guidelines for Implementing and Maintaining Virtual Reference Services," which were subsequently revised in 2010. The new guidelines define "virtual reference" services as those taking place electronically, in which computer technology is used to initiate and further the interaction without face-to-face or phone contact. Virtual reference can take place with any of the following technologies:

- *email*
- *chat/instant messaging*
- *video conferencing* (e.g., the iPhone's FaceTime option)
- *voice over IP* (e.g., Skype)
- *cobrowsing*

RUSA advised library administrators to consider virtual reference services as a "long-term commitment to the targeted community"; not a "fringe service," but one that can become a "natural part of the institution's reference services."

Following up on RUSA's 2010 revision of its guidelines for virtual reference, City University of New York professor Howard Schwartz published an article titled "The Application of RUSA Standards to the Virtual Reference Interview" (2014), in which he discusses the practical application of the RUSA guidelines to email and chat reference service. Schwartz cites several research studies on the use of virtual contact to provide quality reference services, and notes that the most important behavior in providing good reference service, as noted in the original RUSA guidelines, is *approachability*. Face-to-face contact offers multiple ways of signaling approachability (smiling, nodding, making eye contact, gesturing) that virtual reference providers are denied. Instead, other ways must be implemented, which include advertising the availability of email and chat reference, making online access easy to find, and training staff to answer these questions without more than reasonable delay. But some aspects of the interaction remain the same, says Schwartz; the library staffer should maintain a "cordial and encouraging manner" regardless of whether communicating in speech or in writing. Rephrasing of the question is also appropriate for both modes.

Readers interested in early responses to opportunities afforded by virtual reference are encouraged to read "The Reference Interview: Connecting in Person and Cyberspace," a series of presentations and responses published as proceedings from the 2002 American Library Association annual conference.

⊚ Virtual Reference Technology

Many library patrons, especially those under 50, rely on social networking sites like Facebook, Twitter, and Instagram to communicate with peers. Their high level of comfort with screen communication makes them more likely than other users to contact the library reference desk remotely. Thus, twenty-first-century public-service library staff cannot perform effectively without some understanding of the role the different software and networking options play in the information-seeking behavior of those who prefer to seek information via screen, whether synchronous or asynchronous.

The South Carolina State Library (SCSL) used to do an annual survey that looked at how American libraries were using social networking and media tools for building their patron bases and for communicating with their communities. The most recent survey available (Rogers, 2011) indicates that Facebook is the preferred tool for library outreach, with 88.8 percent of libraries saying they use it. Figure 3.2 illustrates that survey.

According to the SCSL survey, the (distant) second preferred tool is Twitter, followed closely by blogging. About one-third of American libraries use the photo-sharing site Flickr, but only about 20 percent make use of "wiki" tools, which allow user

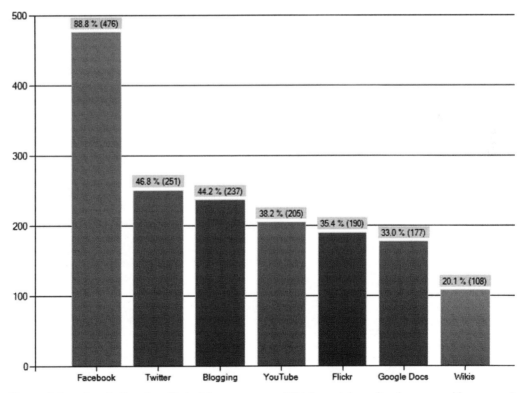

Figure 3.2.   South Carolina State Library survey: Which social media does your library use? http://dc.statelibrary.sc.gov/handle/10827/7271. *Source:* Graph created by Dr. Curtis Rogers, South Carolina State Library

contributions to a knowledge base. Clearly, libraries have a number of well-established options for reaching out. But what about reference services in particular? Can platforms like Facebook and Twitter play a role there? The short answer is, not really. Virtual reference can take place in those contexts, but it's done better with software especially designed for the purpose of receiving and answering questions. Other, more appropriate options for references services are email, text messaging, chat/instant messaging, cobrowsing, and voice over IP (VoIP).

Email

Email is perfect for library reference: it's cheap, widely available, and easy to use. Email contact links can be placed throughout the library's web pages; for users, connecting to reference help can be reduced to a single click, a few words, and a SEND button. Many libraries and other such institutions have email accounts created specifically for particular departments or projects; an institutional name like **reference@publiclibrary.net** makes sense: any reference desk staffer can answer those emails, and answers can be archived. But email is not a new technology, and may even seem antiquated to those born after it became widely used (starting in the 1980s, and picking up speed and finesse in the 1990s). Most of today's university students were born in the 1990s; email has always been part of their world, but they generally prefer other means of virtual contact. Likewise, public library users under 30 might not use email much at all.

Text Messaging

Choosing to text message often seems to vary proportionally with one's age; the younger a person is (starting with pre-teens), the more likely he or she uses text messaging, and the more text messages are sent per day. Whether a library's reference desk can be contacted via text depends on the phone setup; for the most part, texting is still predominantly used between two individuals, rather than between a person and an institution.

Chat/Instant Messaging

The term "instant messaging" (IM) has been around for decades, and the technology for even longer. America Online (AOL) was an early provider of the service, and the way many people discovered it. IM is just like phone texting, only via the Internet. Most libraries in the United States and Canada now offer the option for users to make contact via IM/chat. For library users connecting via library web pages, these descriptors are not even used—users see only a friendly "Ask Us!" invitation and an empty box waiting for their question. Figure 3.3 shows a typical example.

While convenient and easy to use, chat technology has some problems. As already discussed, communication difficulties can arise because chat questions appear on a screen at the reference desk rather abruptly, with no salutation, and the person on the other end has no idea whether the inquirer is male or female, young or old, or even whether they are serious or not. From the perspective of the reference provider, the contact begins in an unhelpful way, with none of the clues that face-to-face interaction provides.

Also, chat technology involves some security risks. Computer viruses and spyware can be transmitted through infected files, so chat users must be cautious about clicking embedded links. Privacy can be compromised as well, because chat windows appear when

Figure 3.3. A typical chat window at a library site

multiple people might have eyes on the screen. And in a university setting, instant messaging could potentially violate FERPA regulations. The Family Educational Rights and Privacy Act of 1974, a federal law, protects the privacy of students over 18 years of age by requiring their consent before their educational records are released to parents or other individuals. IM/chat simply does not allow the responder enough information to judge who is speaking, so problems could arise. Granted, it's not likely that FERPA would be violated by normal reference activity, but the possibility is there.

There are multiple software programs to facilitate chat for the purposes of reference services. Meebo was once popular, but has been out of business for several years; a free service called Trillian can be used as a notification and control system to regulate multiple chat systems through a single source. LibHelp, GoogleTalk, ICQ, Library H3lp, and LibChat are some current options for chat software; each program will have its advocates and detractors, so decision makers should research responses from peers in the reference field as well as the technical specifics of considered programs.

Cobrowsing

Cobrowsing means two people looking at a web page simultaneously, but at a remote distance. The advantage is clear: the patron can watch as the reference desk staffer moves the cursor on the screen and opens new windows. But problems with integration into current operating systems and the library's chat software have made cobrowsing a problematic service option to add.

VoIP

Voice over IP (surely a better name could be assigned?) means using the Internet like a telephone; the popular service Skype is an example. The "IP" (Internet Protocol) can be understood to mean "the computer." Users must connect via computer, and have a microphone for audio and webcam for video on each station; sound is heard through headsets. According to M. Kathleen Kern in her book, *Virtual Reference Best Practices*, patrons can use VoIP to initiate contact with the library's telephone, so "libraries can serve users with VoIP technology without using VoIP themselves" (2009: 53). Skype, which started in 2003, is a free VoIP service with millions of users. However, privacy and security risks are present with any widely used and free service, so reference services providers are encouraged to beware. Kern recommends that you check your institution's policy before committing to a VoIP program.

Whichever software and technology is preferred, reference desk staffers often need a few shortcuts, which is provided by some of the software but not others. If they work in a busy public or college library, staffers need some prescripted replies, or prewritten answers to common questions. Having a macro or some other widget that gives responders the power to send "Hi—I'd be happy to look that up. Please hold for a few minutes . . ." when a new chat window opens up will make both parties happier. The patron gets a quick response, and the information provider can use the time not spent writing that sentence to begin the search. System administrators might even be able to set up an auto-response that achieves the same goal. Many libraries have created "canned" responses that can be copied and tailored to a particular inquiry, and then pasted into a chat window or email.

Library administrators will want to assess the value of any implemented tools; that subject is covered in chapter 5. Kern's book (2009) is recommended for coverage of virtual reference staffing and budgeting concerns, which include marketing virtual reference services. That subject is covered in chapter 4 of this book.

Current Trends in Reference Services

As time passes and libraries adjust to the changes brought by new ideas and new technologies, reference services will certainly be impacted. All change seems disruptive to someone, but administrators can work to minimize that perception. Reference services providers have long known that they no longer exist primarily to provide brief answers to simple questions, à la *Desk Set* (if they ever did), but rather to address complex user needs with a variety of complex tools.

The following are just some of the many issues currently changing in reference services:

- *Diminishing demand.* As users rely on Wikipedia and other online sites reached through Google to answer simple questions, and remotely search full-text databases managed by the library, on-site reference services providers must seek new ways to remain relevant.

- *Changing role of the librarian.* Everyone—library staff and their patrons—knows that the days when library employees primarily just shelved books and shushed people are over. Libraries today are busy places with thousands of tasks being pursued by individuals of all types. Librarians must become experts in evolving technologies or risk losing their relevance, and library staff must remain flexible as their roles change.
- *Demand for 24/7 availability.* Right now, almost all libraries offer reference services (real-time and virtual) only for a limited period of time each day (usually when the library is open). Will the growing demand in other markets for non-stop access alter this paradigm?
- *Changing student demographics.* What role does the reference desk play for non-traditional students? For those taking online classes? Some of these students rely exclusively on document delivery, interlibrary loan, and reference desk chat technology—how can they be served most effectively?
- *E-books, e-journals, and full-text databases.* Gone are the days when the reference desk staffer had a shelf of "ready reference" books that saw frequent use. Now, patrons must be educated in how to search digital formats effectively; that "teaching" has become a regular part of many reference librarians' jobs.
- *Change in library spaces.* A growing trend is to create "learning spaces" and "information commons" in libraries. The traditional reference desk plays a role in these reconfigured spaces, but possibly a new type of service has a place as well?
- *Role of free web resources.* They cannot be dismissed lightly, those thousands and thousands of pages created by dedicated individuals. And, of course, there is Wikipedia. What part can these online resources play in reference services?
- *Change in the nature of questions asked.* As more users practice the do-it-yourself model for finding answers to simple questions, they are coming to the reference desk with more complicated, open-ended questions.
- *Growth of the self-service model.* Many library reference administrators now provide a Frequently Asked Questions (FAQ) page or a link to a Knowledge Base to give patrons the chance to look up the answers themselves. Figure 3.4 shows a typical example.

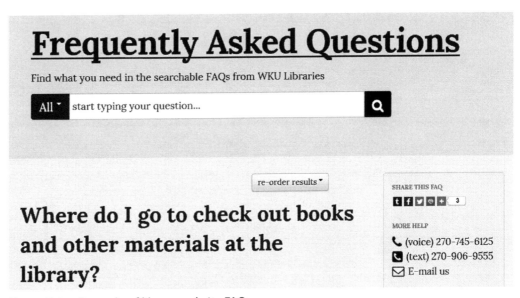

Figure 3.4.   Example of library website FAQ

✇ Key Points

This chapter has provided an in-depth look at some aspects of reference services in practice, and touched on a number of others. In particular,

- Library users rarely ask specifically for what they want, and instead use vague and generalized terminology; thus, the reference desk staffer needs to conduct an effective reference interview. For reference services providers, developing emotional intelligence and learning to be a good listener can enhance reference skills.
- Virtual reference uses complex technology to make access easier for patrons, but communication can be impaired by the lack of visual and tonal cues.
- Reference services are changing right along with libraries as the twenty-first century progresses. How research is done continues to shape the way information providers organize themselves and their services.

The next chapter is all about people; it will cover human resources with regard to reference services.

✇ References

Coleman, Andrew. 2008. *A Dictionary of Psychology*. 3rd ed. New York: Oxford University Press.

Consortium for Research on Emotional Intelligence in Organizations. 2015. "The Mayer-Salovey-Caruso Emotional Intelligence Test (MSCEIT)." http://www.eiconsortium.org/measures/msceit.html.

Covey, Stephen R. 1989. *The 7 Habits of Highly Effective People: Powerful Lessons in Personal Change*. New York: Simon & Schuster.

Dewdney, Patricia, and B. Gillian Michell. 1996. "Oranges and Peaches: Understanding Communication Accidents in the Reference Interview." *Reference Quarterly* 35 (Summer): 520–35.

Gardner, Howard. 1983. *Frames of Mind: The Theory of Multiple Intelligences*. New York: Basic Books.

Goleman, Daniel. 1995. *Emotional Intelligence: Why It Can Matter More Than IQ*. New York: Bantam Books.

Goleman, Daniel. 1998. *Working with Emotional Intelligence*. New York: Bantam Books.

Harmeyer, Dave. 2014. *The Reference Interview Today: Negotiating and Answering Questions Face to Face, on the Phone, and Virtually*. Lanham, MD: Scarecrow Press.

Hendrix, Dana. 2013. "Emotional Intelligence and the Winds of Change in Academic Libraries." *Proceedings from the Association of College & Research Libraries Annual Conference*, Indianapolis, 172–80.

Jordan, Peter J., Claire E. Ashton-James, and Neal M. Ashkanasy. 2006. "Evaluating the Claims: Emotional Intelligence in the Workplace." In *A Critique of Emotional Intelligence: What Are the Problems and How Can They Be Fixed?*, edited by Kevin R. Murphy, 189–210. Mahwah, NJ: Lawrence Erlbaum Associates.

Kern, M. Kathleen. 2009. *Virtual Reference Best Practices: Tailoring Services to Your Library*. Chicago: American Library Association.

Klare, Diane, Melissa Behney, and Barbara Ferrer Kenney. 2014. "Emotional Intelligence in a Stupid World." *Library Hi Tech News* 31, no. 6: 21–24.

Lederer, Naomi. 2001. "E-mail Reference: Who, When, Where, and What Is Asked." *The Reference Librarian* 35, no. 74: 55–73.

Lustberg, Arch, and Dick Walsh. 1989. *Controlling the Confrontation: Arch Lustberg on Effective Communication Techniques*. Chicago: ALA Video.

Masrek, Mohamad Noorman, and Mad Khir Johari Abdulah Sani. 2012. "The Development of Librarian Emotional Assessment Tool." *Proceedings from the 2012 International Conference on Innovation, Management and Technology Research*, Malacca, Malaysia, 679–83.

Matteson, Miriam L., Omer Farooq, and David B. Mease. 2013. "Feeling Our Way: Emotional Intelligence and Information Literacy Competency." *Proceedings from the Association of College & Research Libraries Annual Conference*, Indianapolis, 200–207.

Mayer, John D. n.d. "Emotional Intelligence: Improving Emotional Knowledge and Social Effectiveness." Emotional Intelligence Information, http://www.unh.edu/emotional_intelligence/ei%20Improve/ei%20Rasing%20EI.htm.

McEnrue, Mary Pat, and Kevin Groves. 2006. "Choosing Among Tests of Emotional Intelligence: What Is the Evidence?" *Human Resource Development Quarterly* 17, no. 1 (Spring): 9–42.

Reference and User Services Association. 1996. "Guidelines for Behavioral Performance of Reference and Information Services Professionals." *Reference Quarterly* 36, no. 2 (Winter): 200–203.

Reference and User Services Association. 2010. "Guidelines for Implementing and Maintaining Virtual Reference Services." http://www.ala.org/rusa/sites/ala.org.rusa/files/content/resources/guidelines/virtual-reference-se.pdf.

"The Reference Interview: Connecting in Person and in Cyberspace. Presentations and Responses from the RUSA President's Program, ALA Annual Conference, Atlanta, June 17, 2002." 2003. *Reference and User Services Quarterly* 43, no. 1 (Fall): 37–51.

Rogers, Curtis R. 2011. "Social Media, Libraries, and Web 2.0: How American Libraries Are Using New Tools for Public Relations to Attract New Users—Fourth Annual Survey." South Carolina State Library Digital Collections, http://dc.statelibrary.sc.gov/handle/10827/7271.

Ronan, Jana. 2003. "The Reference Interview Online." *Reference and User Services Quarterly* 43, no. 1 (Fall): 43–47.

Schwartz, Howard R. 2014. "The Application of RUSA Standards to the Virtual Reference Interview." *Reference and User Services Quarterly* 54, no. 1 (Fall): 8–11.

Selby, Courtney. 2007. "The Evolution of the Reference Interview." *Legal Reference Services Quarterly* 26, nos. 1/2: 35–46.

WikiHow. 2015. "How to Be a Good Listener." http://www.wikihow.com/Be-a-Good-Listener.

Managing Staff for Reference Services

ON THE LONG LIST OF THINGS THAT MAKE THE LIBRARY experience unique, the dedication of the extraordinary people who work in libraries must be ranked near the top. Libraries are highly respected institutions in our culture, and that reputation is strongly tied to the distinctive character of the library staff. Many of the library's strongest supporters became so in large part because of their interactions with librarians. Preserving this important library resource is a task as important as any in the profession. Finding and attracting the right employees, training them properly, and motivating them to continue the best traditions of librarianship will be decisive in maintaining libraries as a vital social institution into the future.

Nowhere in a library is staffing more critical than reference services. Reference services staff are often the first line of contact, and their interactions with library users may have a powerful influence on the relationships users form with the library as a whole. Selecting and developing a reference staff can, however, be a challenging task, and one that has become increasingly complex. There are a number of legal aspects that must be considered, and ethical standards that must be maintained, along with increasing awareness of many social justice issues related to human resources. By taking the time to learn some basic procedures and adhere to a few general principles, reference services supervisors can build an outstanding staff that will represent the library in a positive way. Given the potential benefits of an exceptional staff and the negative impact of a poor one, the results are well worth the effort.

⌾ Creating a Staffing Plan for Reference Services

To ensure that you are maximizing the considerable investment you must make in reference services personnel, some careful planning is in order. As in almost any type of administrative planning, the starting point is an examination of the mission and objectives of the organization. This process is described in detail in chapter 5, but, in brief, you must incorporate the goals of the library into those of reference services, then incorporate the goals of reference services into your plans for staffing. If the library is cutting its budget, for example, then consider prudent cost reductions in reference staffing. If the library is focused on upgrading services, a proposal for longer hours of operation might be in order. In addition to providing the rationale for staffing objectives, alignment with organizational goals can help achieve buy-in from library administration, other library departments, and reference staff.

Assessments of reference services are another valuable source of information to guide staffing planning. An assessment may indicate, for instance, that services are understaffed during peak hours, or that additional staffing is required to improve certain services or functions. In some cases, in fact, it may be useful to perform a separate set of assessments specifically designed to evaluate staffing needs. This can take the form of a simple survey, interviews with a sample of library users, or evaluations of the effectiveness of specific reference functions. In other situations, you can obtain all the information you need from existing sources.

Planning and Scheduling Services

The number and types of staffing you will need depends, of course, on the services you plan to provide. There are a wide range of reference services you might offer (see chapter 3 for a detailed discussion), and you should give careful consideration to selecting the most appropriate services for your library. As described above, your organization's mission and objectives provide a useful foundation for your decisions, but ultimately the most important input in choosing services must come from the library's users. Whether your patrons are community users in a public library, the employees of a corporate library, or the students in an academic or school library, the user is the center of every deliberation. Making the best choices for users can, however, be a trickier process than might appear.

There are many sources of user feedback, and all can be helpful. Surveys, interviews, focus groups, and other methods (discussed in chapter 5) can help you discover user preferences and patterns of activity. Keep in mind, though, that user feedback is most useful for telling you how users feel about services already available. Library users can tell you what they do (or don't) like about the service they receive at a reference desk, but they can't tell you that they would like to be able to ask questions through online chat services if they don't know what an online chat service is. It is helpful, then, to try to include items on any user feedback instrument that will reveal what your users are trying to do, and the kinds of problems that impede their efforts. Only by gaining deeper insight into the challenges your users face can you identify services that will help them succeed. By focusing on solving your users' problems, you also gain clarity regarding dismissing services that no longer suit their needs. Services should be retained, not necessarily because they are popular, but because they are the best way to help library users.

This recommendation should not be taken as a dismissal of traditional library services. Library traditions are their own form of comfort—many library patrons actually miss the beautiful old wooden card catalog drawers, and what book lover has not gone to a library in search of a beloved classic they haven't read for many years? While services should not be maintained simply because they have worked in the past, services should never be eliminated simply because they *have* worked for many years. The focus should always be on finding the best solutions to your users' problems and challenges, without overemphasizing novelty at the expense of utility. There is nothing wrong with maintaining traditions, so long as they are the still the best choice for your users. You must also remain alert for useful innovations, which you can accomplish by reviewing journals and blogs, or attending professional conferences and webinars. As long as your decisions remain user-centered and incorporate institutional goals, you will continue to provide the best possible value to both your users and your organization.

In addition to deciding which services you will provide, you must also decide when you will provide them. This means you must determine the hours of operation for each of the separate services, as different services may be useful during different hours. Perhaps, for example, you plan to have librarians provide services at a reference desk for eight hours per day, but you decide that your support staff can offer online chat service for ten hours. Children's programs at a public library might be more popular in after school hours or on the weekend, and staffing levels must reflect this. Making such highly specialized adjustments can complicate the task of staffing reference services, but creates an opportunity to optimize the effectiveness of staffing hours.

Optimizing the Reference Services Staffing Budget

The budget for reference services will determine many of the parameters for reference staffing and activities. It is critical, therefore, that the reference services supervisor have at least a working knowledge of the library budget, and an intimate knowledge of the reference portion of that budget. Furthermore, the supervisor must understand not just the budget totals, but how these totals apply to actual reference operations. If your budget for student assistants in an academic library is $30,000, for instance, how does that translate into hours worked? On some campuses, financial aid funding for student work-study positions is included in the budget, while on others it is not. Using the student assistants as an example, a student employee could be paid $8.00 per hour, but half of that amount might be paid through student financial aid. It is the responsibility of the reference supervisor to understand whether that financial aid is included in the budget or not.

Further complicating staff planning are the many types of employees who can perform reference services. Using the public library as an example, you might have professional librarians, support staff, and volunteers all performing various tasks. As a reference supervisor, you might prefer that general staff answer simple questions but send more complex queries to a librarian. Volunteers may be restricted to support work, such as helping users find a book in the library or bringing supplies to the desk as needed. This means that you must allot hours for each type of employee so that reference operations run smoothly and efficiently. Planning may be further complicated by the need for additional skills, such as answering virtual reference questions through diverse channels like chat, social media, texting, and email. In some cases, developing a scheduling template like the one shown in table 4.1 may be helpful. Even a simple scheduling tool like this can help organize the task of staffing by making it obvious when specific skills are needed, and making it clear which staff members are responsible for specific tasks.

Table 4.1. A Sample Reference Services Schedule Accounting for Multiple Tasks

	9AM–12PM	ASSIGNED	12–3PM	ASSIGNED	3–6PM	ASSIGNED	6–9PM	ASSIGNED
Mon	Desk	Bob	Desk	Allison	Desk	Karl	Desk	Dave
	Virtual	Steve	Virtual	Chris	Virtual	Vickie	Virtual	Nora
	Roaming	Diane	Roaming	Vickie	Roaming	Nora	Roaming	Ellen
Tue	Desk	Cheryl	Desk	Bob	Desk	Allison	Desk	Dave
	Virtual	Steve	Virtual	Vickie	Virtual	Joe	Virtual	Joe
	Roaming	Diane	Roaming	Chris	Roaming	Vickie	Roaming	Ellen
Wed	Desk	Bob	Desk	Janet	Desk	Karl	Desk	Dave
	Virtual	Diane	Virtual	Steve	Virtual	Maria	Virtual	Sara
	Roaming	Joe	Roaming	Maria	Roaming	Vickie	Roaming	Ellen
Thurs	Desk	Ellen	Desk	Bob	Desk	Karl	Desk	Janet
	Virtual	Joe	Virtual	Steve	Virtual	Sara	Virtual	Chris
	Roaming	Diane	Roaming	Maria	Roaming	Tracy	Roaming	Ellen
Fri	Desk	Bob	Desk	Allison	Desk	Janet	Desk	Tracy
	Virtual	Diane	Virtual	Nora	Virtual	Steve	Virtual	Corey
	Roaming	Joe	Roaming	Maria	Roaming	Corey	Roaming	Ellen
Sat	Desk	Allison	Desk	Janet	Desk	Janet	Desk	Karl
	Virtual	Nora	Virtual	Andrea	Virtual	Joe	Virtual	Andrea
	Roaming	Alan	Roaming	Maria	Roaming	Vickie	Roaming	Corey
Sun	Desk	Allison	Desk	Andrea	Desk	Alan	Desk	Karl
	Virtual	Nora	Virtual	Nora	Virtual	Corey	Virtual	Andrea
	Roaming	Maria	Roaming	Alan	Roaming	Chris	Roaming	Corey

A clear, understandable staffing schedule might also help reference supervisors to accurately apportion the number of hours needed for each type of task. Note that in table 4.1, all tasks are assigned during all hours of operation, but in many libraries, this may not be the case. Some tasks require more expertise or education than others, and your staffing schedule can help to determine how many labor hours must be apportioned to each level. Using the sample schedule as an example, you may wish to have librarians with MLS degrees staffing your reference desk to respond face-to-face to clients, but you may find that the technological knowledge required to respond to virtual transactions (such as on-line chat or social media) is better handled by technologically savvy staff members (who could in turn check with librarians for answers to more complex questions). As another example, roving reference assistance could be provided by well-trained student assistants or staff members who help with simple problems throughout the library, sending users to the reference desk for more involved questions. A clear staffing schedule will make these needs more discernible, allowing the supervisor to determine exactly how many labor hours will be required for each employee classification.

Another challenge to staff planning is uncovering and dealing with existing scheduling agreements. This is particularly common when a new supervisor takes over an existing reference operation. Some of these agreements will be explicit and documented, while others may be implicit or unspoken. Detecting every agreement may be difficult, but it is extremely important that the supervisor understand the expectations of the staff. Begin with clearly documented policy statements and employee handbooks. If there is a collective bargaining agreement (i.e., a union contract) in effect, be sure you understand it thoroughly, and seek training specific to your environment. Maintain clear communication with union representatives as well as library administrators.

Some of the most difficult agreements to deal with, though, are the ones that have never been written down and may never have been discussed openly. A staff member may have become used to working only daylight hours for many years, though no actual agreement was ever made. Perhaps a qualified librarian who was either unable or unwilling to work effectively with the public turned out to be very good at performing tasks away from the public—perhaps as a cataloger or systems librarian. A new supervisor who is unaware might then create havoc by placing this librarian back into public contact. In such a case the librarian might feel betrayed, and library users suffer unsatisfactory service. A new reference supervisor may, therefore, wish to invoke a "fresh start" approach, communicating clearly to all staff that previous understandings are nullified, and any special requests should be submitted openly (and preferably in writing). This will eliminate secret arrangements and help to create a more open, equitable work environment.

Once all of this information has been discovered, processed, and incorporated into a staffing schedule, there are still a few issues to grapple with. Consider, for instance, how many days you will have need to replace staff who miss work for sick days, personal days, vacations, sabbaticals, jury duty, emergency leaves, and other interruptions to normal scheduling. Make sure you have a backup plan for covering reference responsibilities during these staffing shortfalls, and then create a backup plan for your backup plan, knowing that you will still find yourself scrambling on occasion to resolve staffing crises. You can, for instance, make arrangements with other departments to cross-train and share employees during times of need. You might also investigate the possibility of bringing on part-time employees who can work on an as-needed basis. Former employees can be invaluable for this sort of thing. Be sure to check with your human resources office or administrators, however, before proceeding—restrictions often apply to part-time hiring.

When all is said and done, though, you may find that even with careful planning, creative budget-stretching, and artful wheeling and dealing with other departments, your staffing levels continue to fall short. If you find yourself in this situation, don't hesitate to make your superiors aware of problems, and work with them to find a resolution. Sometimes additional funding can come from unlikely sources at unlikely times. Even if administrators cannot afford additional staffing, they can frequently draw on their experience to offer highly inventive ways to overcome deficits. Failing this, they may work with you on adjusting hours of operation, types of services offered, and other factors.

◎ Finding the Right People for the Right Jobs

In 2000, influential business writer and researcher Jim Collins studied a special group of businesses. Each of the organizations he studied had transformed themselves over a short period from merely good companies to high-performing, great companies. He decided to look for common factors that might explain what set these extraordinary companies apart—and what he found surprised him. He had expected the transformations to start with a brilliant new organizational vision or mission statement. Instead, he discovered that the leaders who developed great organizations "first got the right people on the bus . . . and the right people in the right seats" (2001: 41) before worrying about where they wanted to drive the bus. Few would argue with the premise that a great staff is indispensable to a great organization. The challenge is to identify and recruit these "right" people of whom Collins speaks. Collins offers few details, suggesting only that you don't hire until you find the "right" person, and that you quickly remove employees who are "wrong."

Many others have studied the effectiveness of a wide variety of selection methods and instruments. Abou-Moghli (2015) found that the use of recruitment and selection procedures in private schools exhibited a significant relationship to institutional excellence. Working in the private sector, Farrell and Hakstian (2001) found that the use of effective selection procedures was related to increases in average sales performance ranging from 14.8 percent to 34.1 percent.

Practices to Avoid

With these and other studies indicating the practical value in using valid selection procedures, it would be natural to assume that every organization adopts the best selection instruments available. This assumption is incorrect. König and colleagues found that "practitioners worldwide often use procedures with low predictive validity and regularly ignore procedures that are more valid" (2010: 17). They reported that organizations regarded accurate results as a minor consideration in choosing a selection procedure. They focused instead on considerations such as the popularity of the instrument with other practitioners, applicant preferences, and cost or time required for the procedure. The regrettable result of this approach is a widespread dependence on a hodgepodge of selection methods, many of which are almost entirely ineffective. Below are just a few of the more common missteps:

- *I just know.* It is not uncommon to hear hiring personnel state that they "just know" which candidates are the best. They will tell you they trust their gut and can pick out a good candidate 15 seconds into an interview. Research indicates that almost all hiring personnel use intuition to some degree to assess an employment candidate, even though they understand that intuition is vulnerable to biases and rater errors (Myers, 2002). But according to Ames et al. (2010), the confidence that assessors have in their intuitive judgments has no relation to the accuracy of those judgments. In short, assessments based on gut feelings and intuition are not an accurate means of assessing employment candidates.

- *Handwriting.* The use of graphology (handwriting analysis) as a means of assessing applicants remains common, despite lack of evidence to support it. To be clear: there is "virtually no research that supports the use of graphology as an effective selection technique" (Thomas and Vaught, 2001: 35).

- *Education.* Often one of the first criteria chosen to identify promising job candidates, education has been used as an indicator of such qualities as professional knowledge, intelligence, persistence, and critical thinking. Educational attainment may be viewed in terms of total years of education completed, or degrees and certifications awarded. No doubt education is an irreplaceable contributor to personal and professional growth, but care must be taken in using education as an employment selection instrument. Since the seminal 1971 Supreme Court decision in *Griggs v. Duke Power*, employers may be expected to provide support for the relationship of educational requirements to actual job performance. A doctoral degree may, for example, be a legitimate requirement to teach a university course in advanced physics, but less so for an employee whose duties are restricted to reshelving books. The *Griggs* decision was related to the use of educational degrees as a subtle means of excluding minorities from employment, but research also indicates that the use of education for hiring assessment is often not useful as a general requirement (Hunter and Hunter, 1984). Only when education is tied directly to a specific job requirement is it a good predictor of performance.

- *Unstructured interviews.* Even the ubiquitous job interview can lead to incorrect perceptions of a job candidate when used improperly. The most common form of interview is what is known as an "unstructured interview"—that is, an interview carried out as a simple conversation between the candidate and one or more hiring personnel. The problem with these open conversations is that they allow interviewers to have a friendly chat with candidates they like, but engage in more formal, and even confrontational, interactions with candidates who seem different. This biased approach opens the door to a wide range of personal prejudices and misconceptions. A much better approach is the use of the structured employment interview (discussed later in this chapter).

Best General Practices

With so much potential to choose staff the wrong way, it may appear that there is little room to find a right way. Nothing could be further from the truth. While it is true that there can never be a magic method of choosing perfect employees every time, there are valid techniques to select staff in ethical, effective, and legally acceptable ways. Below are a few general principles that can help to keep the selection process moving in a positive direction:

- *Strategic Alignment.* As noted throughout this chapter, every phase of staffing and supervision should ideally be aligned with organizational objectives and standards. When the activities of reference services are aligned with the broader goals of the library or organization, the reference staff tends to be more innovative, flexible, and engaged. When staff are valued as contributors to the success of the library as a whole, in other words, their focus will tend to rise above day-to-day job duties. Staff with a positive work attitude often broaden their role to fill many needs throughout the library, and bring a more positive approach to dealing with library users.

- *Evidence-based practice.* There are many studies that support the use of valid selection methods to select staff. These studies indicate that organizations using evidence-based employee selection methods are more effective and productive (for example, see Terpstra and Limpaphayom, 2012). The methods discussed in this chapter provide a number of valid options you can incorporate into your own selection procedures.

- *Respectful practices.* There is probably no more important principle in the field of human resources management than treating employees (and job candidates) with respect and consideration at all times. Sadly, some hiring personnel still hold to the old mythology of the eager job seeker willing to undergo any level of abuse and humiliation on the slim chance of getting hired. Most supervisors are more enlightened, however, and understand that good employees, and in particular good library employees, are an asset and should be treated as such. Blogger Emily Weak (2014) maintains an ongoing survey of library job seekers; she reports that communication is a particularly important issue for job applicants. Keep in mind that it costs nothing to inform your applicants of the timeline of the selection process, and doing so can bring some relief to anxious applicants awaiting the result. Weak also suggests offering feedback to applicants if possible, and making the entire process a positive experience to the greatest extent possible. Applicants are expected to behave in a courteous, respectful manner when applying for a job, and it seems only fair to expect an equal level of professionalism and civility from the employer.

Getting Ready for the Hiring Process

The broad principles of selection discussed above will provide a firm foundation on which to build an excellent reference staff. The next step involves making decisions on the positions you wish to fill. You will need to determine what needs to be done, and the kind of person that can best do this for you. Although seemingly simple, this task can become a highly involved activity requiring costly consultants and vendors, or it may be manageable through a smaller and more casual process. The difference is largely one of scale—larger operations like major university libraries or large urban public library systems may have advanced needs and challenges that require highly developed human resources systems, but the needs of smaller libraries may be more straightforward. This chapter assumes an approach somewhere between the two extremes—if you are working in a large library system, there is likely a human resources department that will control almost every aspect of the hiring process, while a library with only a few employees will have little hiring to worry about. Any person called upon to take part in hiring for reference services should, however, have a practical understanding of at least the basic steps in the hiring process.

Performing a Job Analysis

Properly done, the hiring process begins with a job analysis. Job analysis involves a careful examination of all the duties and requirements for each position in the organization. It is an extremely important part of the hiring process because the results will be used to create job descriptions, job postings and advertisements, training programs, and performance management systems. In a large organization, this process might be performed by a costly external consulting group, though the expense would be beyond the means of most libraries. In other organizations, the responsibility may fall to the human resources department—if you have a human resources department in your library, find out if such an analysis has been done, and, if it has, how it would apply to positions in reference services.

In many libraries, however, supervisors and other administrators must work through this process independently. Performing the job analysis in the most thorough manner possible will pay benefits in the long run, so it is important to commit to the process. Gather as much relevant data and information as possible. You can use old job descriptions, interview current staff and supervisors, and review any institutional documents available. It is also helpful to look over recent assessments and evaluations of reference services. Assessments will help identify needed changes to services, which could, of course, drive changes to reference staffing. Researching the staffing practices of libraries similar to your own can be another rich source of information, allowing comparison to benchmarks and providing fresh ideas for improvement. Below are several examples of the kinds of information that might be collected for a job analysis:

- *What tasks need to be done?* Use all sources at your disposal to find out what needs to be done on the job, in exhaustive detail. Talk to your staff and make them active participants in the analysis. This includes both mental and physical tasks, as well as tasks that are done only occasionally (monthly, seasonally, etc.). Do not limit yourself to what is being done currently—also consider what *should* be done, incorporating feedback from surveys and other assessments to keep jobs relevant to current needs.
- *How are those tasks done?* Determine the methodology used to perform tasks, along with the tools and resources required. Be specific, outlining every step for every task. This is also the time to decide if these tasks are being performed in the most effective and efficient way—if not, now is the time to consider adjustments.
- *Is this job necessary?* Because of the always-present possibility of budget cuts and cost reductions, each position must be reviewed completely and consistently to confirm that it still represents the best use of tight staffing budgets. This means deciding if specific jobs are still relevant, but it also means prioritizing specific tasks to identify the most critical aspects of each position. Be prepared to defend your decisions to superiors in the most objective terms possible, citing key performance statistics and significant accomplishments.
- *What kind of person can best do this job?* If you are to get the right people for reference services, you need to be able to identify them when you find them. This requires that you accurately describe in detail the kinds of knowledge, skills, abilities, and other qualifications needed to perform the job to acceptable standards. This description might include education, experience, certifications, specific task proficiencies, and personal characteristics.

To keep the job analysis on track, remember that you are collecting information about the job, not about the staff members who do it. The distinction sometimes reveals itself when examining tasks performed by particularly talented or experienced employees— some employees may develop ways of working based on extraordinary abilities, or may take on responsibilities outside the normal range of the position. It is important to remain focused on actual job responsibilities. Also, be aware that a job analysis is sometimes a mandated legal requirement or a contractual obligation for the organization, and could involve specific conditions concerning data collection or other parts of the job analysis procedure. Always check with your library administration to discover such requirements before undertaking a job analysis.

Creating Job Descriptions

The information gathered in the job analysis can now form the basis of a job description—a detailed written summary of a specific job. Creating the job description allows for several benefits: it requires all responsible parties to agree on the definition of the job. Sometimes this process can be contentious, but the resulting document will help employees understand what is expected of them, and help supervisors know what they should ask of their staff. Additionally, the job description is valuable in recruiting the right people for the job, as it will, in turn, become the basis for job postings and advertisements. Job descriptions can also provide legal documentation for such issues as required candidate qualifications, or essential tasks and responsibilities for a specific position. It is critical, therefore, that job descriptions are complete, accurate, and current. At the minimum, the following items should be included:

- *Title*. The job title should describe the primary function of the job, but it should be kept short and to the point. It is not necessary to include every task or responsibility— just make the nature of the job as clear as possible using only a few words.
- *Details*. A number of small but relevant details should be documented in the job description, for example, the department in which the job is based, the person to whom the employee will report and, if available, the job identification number. The description should also include the type of job (e.g., salaried or hourly, staff or faculty, exempt or non-exempt). Other information can be added as appropriate, such as salary and benefits, application deadline, and estimated starting date.
- *Position summary*. A brief description (usually one to three short paragraphs) of the position in narrative form should provide a broad picture of the nature of the job, including information such as essential functions, primary areas of responsibility, and unusual aspects of the job that you wish to highlight. Keep in mind that the summary is frequently copied verbatim to create job postings and advertisements.
- *Tasks, duties, and responsibilities*. A list of what is done on the job must contain all of the primary responsibilities, but avoid including so much detail that the document becomes confusing or off-putting. The most important functions should be listed first, and it is best to begin each statement with an active verb (e.g., "assists researchers," or "creates research guides"). The list is frequently presented in bullet points—in some cases larger bullets are primary responsibilities, followed by smaller bullets for detailed tasks related to each.
- *Job qualifications*. The types of knowledge, skills, abilities, and other characteristics required of employees should be listed. Each requirement must be strictly job-related. Asking for library staff having the physical ability to push book carts and lift volumes to upper shelves is reasonable, but demanding that candidates be able to bench-press at least 250 pounds is not. Similarly, ask only for the level of education needed to complete the job. Many employers use educational degrees as a proxy for intelligence or other virtues, but this is a dangerous assumption to make without

job-related evidence to support it. Finally, be sure to include qualifications that are truly relevant, with due consideration to the available labor pool for the job. Do not create so many demands that you have little chance of finding good applicants. It might be helpful to split qualifications into "required" qualifications that are absolutely necessary to performing the job, and "preferred" qualifications that are helpful but not necessary. Even the preferred qualifications should, however, be directly related to job performance.

- *Working conditions.* This section could be added to describe unusual conditions or circumstances that employees will encounter in the position. This may include positive aspects of the job (such as paid travel to other countries, or a desirable location), as well as aspects that might be regarded as challenging (such as working with hazardous materials, or living in a politically unstable country). It could also deal with general work conditions such as stress levels or seasonal workloads.

Finally, here are a few general tips that will help in writing effective job descriptions. First and foremost, carefully avoid making good candidates feel excluded. Use language that is respectful in terms of gender and culture, and don't be too rigid in your requirements— leave enough flexibility to allow for the full range of people who might do the job well, if in different ways and coming from different backgrounds. Avoid buzzwords and imprecise language such as *self-starter, highly motivated,* and *dynamic.* They sound meaningful, but they are useless as real job qualifications. It is far better to focus on specific behaviors or abilities than vague character qualities. Finally, when possible avoid library jargon (indexes, serials, stacks) and acronyms (OPAC, LIS, ILL).

Recruiting Candidates

When you have developed a plan for hiring staff and have created accurate descriptions of the jobs you need to fill, it is time to recruit candidates. All of the preparation done to this point will be tested in the real world of the job market. If you have not yet done so, check with appropriate library administrators or human resources personnel prior to undertaking an employment search. Hiring an employee is a big step—you are obligating your organization to a major commitment of salary and other forms of compensation that may stretch over many years or decades. In addition, the search process itself could, if flawed, undergo court challenges for unfair or illegal hiring practices. Be sure you have carefully considered every aspect before proceeding.

In order to reach potential job candidates, you should create one or more job postings or advertisements. If you have performed a thorough job analysis and used the results of this analysis to build accurate, up-to-date job descriptions, then creating a job posting should be a relatively easy task. You can simply draw the relevant information from your job description. The content of your posting will vary according to the type of job you wish to fill, and the nature of the media you use to advertise it. Your first decision, then, is the type of staff you need to perform the job in question. Depending on the type of library and the nature of reference services, any of the following might be possible:

- *Academic and school librarians.* Many educational libraries have specific requirements for their reference librarians. Librarians serving K–12 students must normally possess a specific state certification. Colleges and universities usually require that their librarians complete a Master of Library Science (MLS) degree from an ALA-accredited institution. Many universities also require a second degree in a subject specialization. Academic librarians may have faculty status, including tenure, and as such must fulfill specific requirements for teaching, service, and academic publishing. These requirements are often established by state law or by the policies of an institution, and are therefore rarely open to negotiation.

- *Professional staff librarians.* Most public libraries and many academic libraries hire their librarians as professional staff. This often requires an MLS degree, though in some cases a related degree or equivalent experience as a librarian may suffice. Librarians at this level may be hired full or part time, and while they are most often salaried, they may work on an hourly basis.

- *Library Staff.* Demanding an MLS degree for each staff position in the library would be wasteful and unnecessary. There are always many important functions that require educated, capable employees, but not necessarily employees with a library science education or background. In reference services, support staff can organize schedules, move and reshelve reference materials, and supervise student assistants. These invaluable support staff members can make the difference between good and great reference operations.

- *Interns.* Libraries on or near a campus with a library science program are fortunate to have another option for excellent, well-educated, highly motivated staff, obtainable for a reasonable cost. Library science interns are often graduate students (though some are undergraduates) willing to provide services for a semester or more in order to gain experience in a real library workplace. They bring a fresh perspective from their coursework and research, and many have completed enough coursework to answer at least basic questions at a reference services desk. Interns can also be a wonderful way to approach succession planning—exceptional performance by an intern often translates into permanent employment in the library.

- *Student assistants.* For academic libraries, school libraries, and some public libraries, undergraduate or high school student employees may be a great way to get work done at low cost. Undergraduate students can be bright, willing employees who help with reshelving reference books, lead library users to the materials they are seeking, and take on many of the time-consuming chores that can devour a librarian's time. Students approved for work study often receive part of their pay from educational grants or other forms of financial aid, providing additional savings. Do keep in mind that employers must accommodate class schedules and other school obligations when working with student employees, and there are some tasks not appropriate for them.

- *Volunteers.* Libraries are regarded with great warmth by many of the people who use them. This affection often rises to the level of a willingness to volunteer to work at the library. For some, this experience answers their curiosity about what it would be like to work in a library. For others, it seems to be a higher calling to service. Whatever the motivation, library volunteers can inspire the library's employees and users alike. Volunteers provide countless benefits to their libraries, from reshelving books to arranging and hosting events. They are an asset to be appreciated, acknowledged, and, whenever possible, recruited.

Successfully recruiting the various types of employees described above demands that an employer identify the best way to reach each of them. You might first consider the geographic scope of your search. Posting for a tenure-track faculty librarian in an academic environment would call for a national, or even international, search. You may, on the other hand, find a great group of candidates for an office support position with no more than a brief job posting on the library website. Regardless of the type of position, however, you should always widen your net enough to draw a broad, diverse applicant pool. Many libraries struggle, for example, to recruit minority and international applicants. This is especially unfortunate in that a diverse library staff can provide a richer view of the world so valuable to a library's curious patrons. Seize every opportunity, therefore, to discover new media outlets and alternate forms of communication to reach a larger labor market.

Deciding on the right communication package for your purposes is crucial, and there is no fixed formula. It is important to find out how potential employees see the world— how they prefer to communicate, the ways in which they search for information, and what they find motivating. You can review library professional literature for suggestions, and you can collect ideas from other libraries. It is likely that the most productive method, however, is to ask. Ask your current employees, or consider incorporating a few relevant questions into employment interviews. Once you have a good idea of how to reach your target audience, pick the best alternatives for communication and proceed. The results will indicate the effectiveness of your plan, so track them carefully and keep notes for future employee searches. Some of the most popular methods of advertising job openings are listed below:

- *Internal candidates.* The simplest, least expensive method of posting a job opening is within your own library or organization. Internal candidates are always worth considering—they know the library, and the library knows them. Reaching them often requires nothing more than posting a notice on bulletin boards or through an internal email. Unless there is a pressing reason to do so, however, this should never be the only source of candidates, and internal applicants should not be under the impression that they will always be hired over external applicants. Also, be aware that internal hiring is often closely controlled by institutional policies.
- *Posting through the library.* Another cheap and obvious method of advertising a job opening is through your own library. Job announcements placed throughout the library and posted on the library website will attract library users, and this may be a positive thing for some positions. It is also wise to consider, though, that candidates recruited in this way are often library users and patrons—people who have an existing relationship with the library, and people you might see for many years into the future. As with all candidates, they must be treated with empathy and respect.
- *Periodicals/newspapers/journals.* In the past, newspapers and other print publications were the medium of choice for job advertisements. As regrettable as this may be for some, there are better strategies for reaching employment candidates, particularly younger candidates.
- *Online job sites.* At this time, the most popular method of reaching a wide audience of potential applicants is the use of online job sites. The largest of these are the general-interest sites like Indeed, Monster, and CareerBuilder. These sites may be helpful for finding good candidates for support positions and general employment, as well as librarians. For government library jobs, government websites are an effective alternative. To find librarians and library specialists (such as catalogers or library systems programmers), try the websites of professional organizations like the American Library Association or the Special Libraries Association. Most of these sites charge a fee based on the number of words and the length of time

the ad runs. Other options include the websites of library science programs and library-related listservs.

- *Word of mouth.* Depending on word of mouth to pass news of a job opening may seem archaic, limiting, and a violation of the principles of inclusiveness discussed only a few paragraphs previously. It does, however, have its place. Many librarians have extensive professional networks built through library organizations, committee work, former colleagues, old library school acquaintances, and other sources. Recruiting through these connections can bring in qualified, experienced candidates who are active in their profession and can work well with colleagues. This is a valuable recruiting method, but, as with internal recruiting, it should not be your *only* method.

- *Social media.* Given the unavoidable spread of social media into every form of human interaction, it should come as no surprise that the use of social media for employment recruiting is on the rise. Sites such as LinkedIn and other professional networking sites are particularly useful for this purpose. Before jumping into this new trend, however, consider the legal ramifications of having access to candidate photographs and personal posts—some of the information commonly shared on social media is not appropriate for employment deliberations. Each social media application has different procedures and policies, so review carefully before proceeding. It is best to pass over systems that could place your organization at risk.

Assessing Candidates

Once you have obtained an acceptable applicant pool for your employee search, it is time to sort through the applications to identify the best candidates. This is a deceptively difficult task, bristling with legal, ethical, and perceptual implications. As described earlier in this chapter, the use of evidence-based selection practices is an effective means of avoiding difficulties. Another key strategy is ensuring that each applicant is evaluated by the same standards and treated in the same respectful manner. The assessment of candidates amounts to nothing less than fortune-telling, and the candidates' perception of fairness may well begin with the type of crystal ball you choose. It is extremely important, therefore, to use assessment techniques that are valid, ethical, and make sense to your applicants.

Reviewing Submitted Materials

The best way to begin an assessment of potential candidates is with a careful review of the materials you have asked them to submit. The complexity of this task is strongly correlated to the complexity of the job. Reviewing applications for a student assistant position is often simply a matter of making sure the applicant really is a student, and checking references to find out how the student interacted with former teachers or employers. For a tenure-track faculty librarian at a university, the materials will be more involved, including, at the very least, letters of reference, transcripts, extensive curriculum vitae (CV), and a cover letter. For all positions, begin by developing a checklist or digital system confirming that all materials have been received, then begin examining materials to identify candidates possessing all the requirements for the position. Any applicants who do not meet every requirement can be immediately eliminated from further consideration.

For most jobs, this review of materials is also a good time to rate candidates on the relative merits of their qualifications. This task can, of course, become complicated very quickly. Some jobs, particularly multifaceted positions such as reference librarian, may have dozens of interrelated qualifications, and some may be hard to rate in an equitable manner across all applicants. One useful approach is to create an anchored rating system for each major job qualification. A basic rating scale for one qualification—a candidate's level of work experience—is shown in table 4.2. In this example, the candidate's experience may be assigned a rating of 1 through 5, with 5 being the highest. For each level, there is an anchor—a tangible example of the kind of experience required to be rated at that level. In this case, a candidate who has done volunteer work in a library would rate a 2, while a reference librarian with five years' experience would receive a rating of 4. Such a rating scale will allow you to rank the qualifications of candidate, but do keep in mind that the resulting data is ordinal, not interval—in other words, the levels follow in order from 1 to 5, but a rating of 5 is not necessarily 5 times better than a rating of 1.

The Structured Interview

What, then, are the best applicant assessment tools for the library environment? One of the best predictors of job performance, unfortunately, is general mental ability (intelligence). The problem is that many general mental ability tests exhibit a greater or lesser degree of bias—they have been shown to have a negative impact on protected populations. Research indicates, though, that another good predictor of job performance, the structured job interview, provides a serviceable measure of general mental ability. A well-constructed interview can, in other words, not only obtain the candidate's answers to job-related questions, but will also act as an indicator of general mental ability, as well as emotional intelligence (Kluemper et al., 2015). The structured interview does require careful preparation, but the results are so useful that it is generally worth the effort. Below are some steps to get you started:

1. *Base your questions on the job analysis.* Identify job-related requirements that may not show up on résumés, CVs, or employment application forms. This may include employee attitudes about such subjective issues as willingness to work in a team environment, or level of comfort serving the public in stressful situations.

Table 4.2.   An Anchored Rating Scale for Candidate Work Experience

RATE THE CANDIDATE BASED ON HIS/HER PREVIOUS WORK EXPERIENCE.	
RATING	INDICATORS
5	Has held a supervisory or administrative position in reference services
4	Has worked as a reference librarian, over four years
3	Has worked as a reference librarian, three years or less
2	Library experience as a volunteer or student assistant
1	No experience working in a library
N/A	Not applicable or insufficient data

2. *Ask open-ended questions.* Avoid questions that only require a yes or no answer. Ask candidates to explain how they would approach a job responsibility, or give an example of a time they have dealt with a particular work-related situation. Depending on the position, you could ask questions that will test the depth of the candidate's knowledge and thinking about a challenging work topic, such as a comparison of the benefits of digital and paper resources.

3. *Decide who will participate.* The primary goal in creating a structured interview is to make the process identical for each candidate. This means the same person or persons should ask the questions each time. If multiple interviewers are asking questions, some experts even suggest that the same interviewers ask the same questions for all candidates.

4. *Use structured scoring as well.* Not only the questions but the scoring of the interviews must be identical for each candidate. Many factors can affect interview responses, but you can create a scoring guide that will keep responses tied to a common standard. The anchored rating scale discussed earlier in this chapter could easily be applied in this situation as well. An example of a rating scale for an interview response is shown in table 4.3. In this case, a poor or incomplete response rates a 1, whereas a candidate who completely understands the process and its implications receives a rating of 5.

Work Samples

Another popular assessment instrument for personnel selection in reference services is the work sample. It should be obvious that the work sample can only be used for work the candidate already knows how to do. In an academic environment, for example, reference librarians are often asked to deliver an instructional presentation as a part of the selection process, to ensure they possess the necessary communication skills. In other environments, library candidates may be asked to role-play a reference transaction, or to

Table 4.3.   An Anchored Rating Scale for Interview Responses

RATE THE CANDIDATE ON HIS/HER RESPONSE TO THE PROMPT: *Please describe the process you would use to assist a library patron asking for help at the reference service desk.*	
RATING	**INDICATORS**
5	Shows awareness that the reference librarian represents the library as a whole, and that the quality of the user's overall experience will affect the user's relationship to the library
4	Shows awareness of the reference transaction as more than an exchange of information—it is an interpersonal experience
3	Would ask additional questions to determine what the reference user is really looking for, and the purpose the information must fulfill
2	Simple transactional response, would answer the question asked
1	Response unsure and incomplete; candidate does not know how to respond to a request for reference services
N/A	Not applicable or insufficient data

answer questions typical of those that might arise at a reference desk. Even volunteers or student assistants might need to perform a work sample showing that they can lift heavy books onto upper shelves, or push a full cart of books. When designing a work sample test, be sure that the work is an essential function of the job, and that it involves an ability or skill that can legitimately be expected pre-employment.

Overlapping Assessments

The assessment methods described above are each helpful independently, but the best way to assess employment candidates is to use multiple, sometimes overlapping, methods. This strategy, sometimes called "triangulation," refers to using multiple assessment measures to build a clearer picture of the candidate's potential to successfully perform the duties of the position. An illustration of this principle is shown in figure 4.1, where three types of assessment are performed: the candidate's work history, professional judgment, and job-related abilities. Note that there may be overlap in the assessments, where work history tells you something about the candidate's abilities or sense of judgment.

The various factors may all be considered equally, or greater weight may be given to a specific criterion—in this case, for example, you might believe that professionalism and judgment are more important than the candidate's work history or skills. In practical terms, this distinction can be accomplished by assigning weights to each rating and adding them up to determine the best candidate. You can also assess your candidates through a system of "multiple hurdles." Using this system, you would first determine a cut-off for ratings on an assessment with a pass or fail rating. If, for instance, the position requires a library science degree, only candidates with such a degree would pass through. Similar cutoffs could be set for each assessment. Some practitioners use this method to winnow

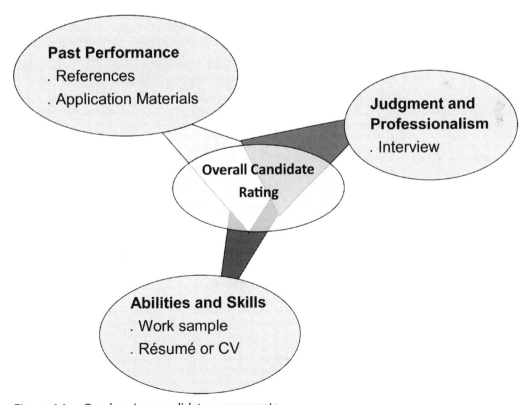

Figure 4.1.   Overlapping candidate assessments

the applicant pool down to a small group, and this group will then be brought in for a final interview or other selection procedure.

The suggestions above are among the more practical, cost-effective options for assessing employment candidates, but there are many other possibilities. No matter how careful or thorough your assessments, though, there will eventually come the moment when you or your selection committee must make that final employment decision. Supervisors can work hard to make the selection process fair, understandable, and objective, but at the end of the day the employment decision comes down to a leap of faith. You can never really be certain which candidate is the best choice in a specific situation—over time, however, a rational, ethical selection program will yield the best employees, the highest morale, and the greatest degree of protection against legal challenges.

◎ Training the Reference Services Staff

When you have hired new staff for reference, you want to give them the best chance to succeed in their new position. A well-planned, effective program of orientation and training is certainly the first and most important step to accomplish this. Unfortunately, as with so many supervisory and administrative tasks in a library, training is often approached in a fairly lackadaisical manner. The entire training program may amount to little more than introducing the new staff member to a couple of coworkers, then plunking them on the reference desk to observe briefly before leaving them to their fate. A better, more organized approach can help to improve the capabilities of new staff and librarians significantly, and it will make the adjustment smoother and more comfortable. Remember, just as you are observing your new employees and forming judgments based on what you see, so your new employees are making judgments about you and your library. This first impression could dramatically affect the morale, motivation, turnover, and performance of your staff.

Begin developing your training program by referring to organizational goals and the needs of reference services. Determine how the new employee can help the library reach these goals, then consider how best to explain each objective and teach trainees to perform specific tasks and duties. Be clear on the results you expect of training. Document the types of knowledge that trainees should absorb, the skills they should master, and the responsibilities they must be able to fulfill.

When you have decided on the content you need to deliver, develop a reasonable schedule for doing so. Divide the training appropriately—you may, for example, wish to train a reference librarian on library resources in one session, digital systems in another, and service practices in a third. Make training sessions reasonable in length, and avoid crushing trainees with too much information at one time. Also, give your new employees time to absorb what they have learned, allowing them to practice repeatedly before sending them off to their new responsibilities. Below are several additional issues you should consider as you prepare new hires to become productive, successful members of your team:

- *Orientation.* Beginning a new job is always stressful, so do everything you can to make the first few days as painless—even enjoyable—as possible. If the trainee is alone and not part of a group of new employees, consider assigning a mentor or companion who will accompany the employee through filling out employment paperwork and navigating initial tasks like setting up email and voicemail. It might be helpful to arrange a lunch with some friendly coworkers, and to schedule meetings with experienced colleagues who can offer advice as needed. Create a packet with necessary information, forms and, if the new employee has just moved into the area, perhaps tips on adjusting to life in your city.

- *Individualized training.* Even if you are training a group of new employees, consider the individual differences among them. Customize training not only for the needs of a specific job, but also to reach the individual before you. Different people have, for instance, different learning styles. Some learn verbally, some are better with written materials, and others prefer hands-on work. Different cultures may also experience learning in different ways, and people of different age groups may have drastically different perceptions of training. Keep your training methods flexible enough to reach out to all your trainees.

- *Coaches and mentors.* A wonderful way to individualize the training function is through mentoring. Personalized mentoring and coaching can certainly help new employees to adjust to their surroundings, and the process is beneficial well beyond the training and probationary period. Having a supportive mentor who is available to answer questions, offer advice, and help to overcome obstacles can make all the difference in a new employee's job performance—in some cases it can, in fact, be the central turning point in a person's career.

- *Assessment.* It is highly beneficial to assess the effectiveness of training. While no one wants to receive bad reports on the quality of their training sessions, valid feedback can help any trainer improve the quality of their efforts. Test to make sure you are accomplishing the outcomes you set for yourself when planning training. You can survey the trainees' perceptions of their training, you can test them on training content, or you can track their work to determine the effects of training on actual job performance.

◎ Supervising Reference Staff

Thousands of books have been written about supervising, managing, and leading others. Many of them are superb, and reading at least a few of the top authors on the subject (Peter Drucker, Stephen R. Covey, Warren Bennis) can help any supervisor to expand their knowledge and expertise. Supervising reference services, however, is usually a relatively straightforward task, and relies largely on a few basic supervisory skills. Some of the broader supervisory responsibilities for reference services are discussed in chapter 5, but the following sections deal specifically with supervising subordinates, with a focus on two of the most important skills for any supervisor: workplace communication and performance management.

Communicating with the Reference Staff

Communicating effectively with each member of the reference staff should be your highest priority as a supervisor. It is only natural that some of your subordinates will be easier to communicate with than others, but it is crucial that you make your best attempt to reach everyone on your staff. It is also important to make sure the communication goes both ways—the goal is to develop healthy workplace relationships in which everyone can communicate freely, professionally, and without fear.

One way to encourage a positive environment for communication is individualizing communication to suit the many types of people on the reference staff. A library can be a wonderfully diverse setting, with people from many cultures, academic disciplines, backgrounds, and ages—so one size will rarely fit all when dealing with the reference staff. Younger employees may, for example, prefer to send messages through social media rather than email. Others may prefer face-to-face or even paper communication. You can't always satisfy every preference in every situation, but where possible, be flexible in your approach.

Another benefit of personalizing communication is the ability to hold meaningful, authentic discussions with your subordinates. There are few situations in which people are highly moved and motivated by cookie-cutter mass communication. Working one-on-one can bring your staff into closer contact with their responsibilities, their work environment, and often with their colleagues and coworkers. Good communication across the reference staff can help to build an effective team atmosphere, eliminating "us-versus-them" interactions among cliques and groups.

A final point about communication with reference staff: it should be purposeful. This should not be taken to imply that you only speak to your staff when you have something to gain, and it certainly does not preclude personal interactions and discussions. When you are discussing substantive work-related matters, though, your communication must be more organized, with a clear idea of what you wish to say and what you want to accomplish when you say it. It must be expressed more professionally than a simple personal interaction. You also need to permit the person with whom you are communicating to express their views openly, working to reach consensus and a mutually agreeable outcome to the greatest extent possible. Having concluded your communication, show that you respect the other party by taking action on what you have discussed, then update everyone concerned. A communication process of this type will not, unfortunately, guarantee that each interaction will be a victory, but it will give you the best possible likelihood of successfully building positive relationships with, and among, your staff.

Meetings are an entirely different approach to workplace communication, with a separate set of benefits and pitfalls. Few people like workplace meetings, and many staff members actively avoid them if possible. A well-run meeting can, however, provide valuable team input, help to build consensus on difficult issues, and sometimes they even turn out to be enjoyable. Suggested steps for making your meetings productive and fulfilling include:

1. *Agenda*. It is always best to create an agenda describing each topic you wish to discuss in the meeting. Prioritize all items, and allot a specific amount of time for each. Avoid trying to accomplish too much in a single meeting—the attendees will become tired and impatient, leading to poor decisions. For the same reason, try to limit meetings to an hour or less.
2. *Preparation*. Even if you are busy, take the time to prepare thoroughly for the meeting. Prepare slides or copies of materials to be covered. Make sure you have all the information you will need. For meetings of reference services staff, it is also important to remember that you need to find someone to cover reference or digital services while the meeting is taking place.
3. *Attendance*. Meetings in which the attendees are expected to contribute in an interactive manner should probably be limited to about eight to ten people. Make sure all attendees have a reason to be there and can make a viable contribution to the discussion.

4. *Momentum.* Use your agenda as a guide to stay on topic and on schedule. Be assertive in diverting off-topic conversations to a more appropriate time and place. Assign time limits to speakers if needed, and make sure everyone has an opportunity to contribute to the conversation.

5. *Conclusion.* Allow time at the end of the meeting to summarize what has been discussed, the decisions reached, and items that must be deferred to a future date. It is particularly important to assign tasks—responsibility for each task should be assigned to a specific person. Finally, consider sending out a written summary, with task assignments, after the meeting is over. This will serve as both reminder and documentation of what occurred at the meeting.

Performance Management

Performance management refers to a set of procedures designed to help supervisors and employees work together to produce the best possible job performance. This may include setting goals, evaluating performance, designing professional development plans, and other activities. In many libraries, the human resources department or representative will oversee this function closely, while in others there may be no formal requirements at all. Begin by gathering information about your library's rules and guidelines. There are legal implications for many aspects of performance management, so comply completely with the policies in your organization.

Performance Evaluations

First, a caution about performance evaluations—supervisors and subordinates alike often regard these as among the most stressful, disagreeable tasks they face during the year. It is critical, then, to make the evaluation experience as positive as possible for all concerned. All parties must be clear that the goal of performance evaluations is not to attack or belittle anyone, but to support employees in their efforts to become better at their jobs and more successful in their careers. This begins with an honest assessment of current performance, carried out in the most consistent, objective manner possible. When assessors comport themselves in a fair and respectful manner throughout the performance evaluation process, they give their subordinates the best chance of achieving positive results. The following are key considerations in designing an equitable evaluation:

- *Set clear standards.* It is imperative that the criteria used in performance evaluations are understood clearly by all parties. The job description should, of course, form the basis of all job tasks and responsibilities, and you should have met with your employees at the beginning of the evaluation period to have a detailed discussion of specific goals and objectives. It is best to give your subordinates considerable input in creating their goals. The goals themselves must be measurable, and there should be a written timeline for achieving specific objectives. Above all, remember that you are assessing work performance and observable behaviors, not people or personalities.
- *Track behavior and outcomes.* Evaluations should be based on specific behaviors and work results. This requires good data for all aspects of performance to be evaluated, including detailed records of specific behaviors and outcomes. If a staff member calls in sick too often, for instance, be prepared to report the number of incidents,

the dates, and reasons given. If a reference librarian has given out incorrect information, be prepared to discuss specifics. Consider creating a rating scale for each aspect of performance being evaluated, with specific behaviors or outcomes as examples of each rating level.

- *Hold an evaluation meeting*—evaluations should be discussed in person with employees. This meeting should be held the most positive environment possible. Discuss results in an honest, straightforward manner—be diplomatic and respectful, but do not be evasive or beat around the bush. Begin the discussion with a review of the performance evaluation. Have data to back up statements. Once you have covered the evaluation results, be prepared to move quickly into a discussion of using the results as the basis for a development plan. Work together to establish goals and objectives for the coming evaluation period, and plan to meet regularly throughout the year to discuss progress. Constant communication is vital to the evaluation process—nothing in the performance evaluation should come as a surprise to the employee.

Interventions and Development

Once you have discussed performance with your subordinate, the next step is laying out a plan of development for the coming evaluation period. Regardless of the ratings an employee receives—good or poor—the approach is the same: supervisor and subordinate work together to find ways to reach the next level. While the general approach will always be the same, each plan must be tailored to the specific employee, with every aspect designed to address the unique talents and needs of the individual. The best supervisors recognize the potential of each employee, and will work hard to reveal it. Sometimes this will require persistence and creativity—even the most accomplished librarians and staff sometimes travel a difficult path to excellence. Below are a few suggestions to get you started, but never stop seeking out new ways to develop your staff.

- *Examine the system.* When you notice performance problems, first consider the possibility that the system is at fault. Examine workplace procedures, methods, and equipment. Make sure you are giving your staff the best opportunity to succeed. Even if you find no problems, your subordinates will appreciate the fact that you did not simply assume they were at fault.
- *Training.* Once you have identified developmental needs for one of your employees, training and education should be your next move. This may amount to in-house training sessions to sharpen general skills and abilities, or it might involve arranging formal classes or workshops for your staff. To improve the skills of reference librarians, consider professional and academic conferences or, failing that, webinars or other digital alternatives. Be open and flexible concerning training options—each employee will have different needs.
- *Coaching and mentoring.* When helping your staff improve and develop, nothing replaces the personal touch. Highly successful people in all occupations often refer to early mentoring relationships as the single most important factor in their success. Individual coaching can help improve performance and morale. It can be highly effective in both reducing turnover and facilitating succession planning. It is also a useful way to approach major changes in the workplace—one-on-one mentoring

helps to overcome the many adjustments that must be made to day-to-day procedures to accommodate sweeping organizational change.

- *Motivate your staff.* Contrary to popular belief, raises and other monetary rewards are good motivators only in the short term. The most effective way to motivate employees is to help them understand the importance of the library's mission. Helping your employees reach their career goals is also important, as is respecting the importance of their personal lives. Finally, remember the little things, like praising exceptional efforts publicly, recognizing birthdays and special occasions, and regularly spending time with each individual on your team.

- *Further action.* In the course of working with subordinates, you will occasionally run across those whose performance is exceptionally good or exceptionally poor. The best approach for both is largely the same: make the person aware of where they stand, and work with them on an individual basis to make the needed changes. A great employee is a valued gift you never want to give up, but it is important to help exceptional employees move forward, if they wish to do so, toward greater responsibility and possible promotion, even if this is outside your library. Employees exhibiting chronic performance problems are likewise in need of personalized attention, and you must commit personal time and effort to helping them overcome obstacles. Be compassionate, communicate clearly, and, if persistent efforts to improve do not bear fruit, then proceed to your organization's procedures for corrective action. This may consist of counseling sessions, written warnings, and perhaps even termination. These are drastic measures taken only as a last resort, but this is sometimes more considerate than allowing a bad situation to drag on. Whether working with your top performers or those facing challenges, it is important for you, your subordinates, and your organization to do everything possible for the employees who need your help the most.

⊚ Key Points

Material covered in this chapter will enable a reference services supervisor to build and develop an effective staffing program.

- An effective reference services staffing program must start with an effective staffing plan, incorporating the mission and goals of the library as a whole, and in compliance with the human resources policies of the organization.
- Good hiring decisions are crucial to building a good staff, and should be based on solid evidence and objective candidate assessments, not instinct.
- No matter how talented or motivated your staff, they will not reach their true potential without proper training and development, both during orientation and throughout their careers.
- Improving the job performance of your staff is best approached as a partnership between supervisor and subordinate, working together to form a practical yet creative plan to enhance the employee's contribution to the organization.

The next chapter will further examine supervision of reference services, with a focus on the broader roles of leadership and management.

References

Abou-Moghli, Azzam. 2015. "Recruitment and Selection and Their Effect in Achieving Institutional Excellence." *International Business Research* 8, no. 3: 156–64.

Ames, Daniel R., Lara K. Kammrath, Alexandra Suppes, and Niall Bolger. 2010. "Not So Fast: The (Not-quite-complete) Dissociation between Accuracy and Confidence in Thin-slice Impressions." *Personnel and Social Psychology Bulletin* 46, no. 2: 264–77.

Collins, Jim. 2001. *Good to Great: Why Some Companies Make the Leap . . . and Others Don't.* New York: HarperCollins.

Farrell, Seonaid, and A. Ralph Hakstian. 2001. "Improving Salesforce Performance: A Meta-Analytic Investigation of the Effectiveness and Utility of Personnel Selection Procedures and Training Interventions." *Psychology & Marketing* 18, no. 3: 281–316.

Hunter, John E., and Ronda F. Hunter. 1984. "Validity and Utility of Alternative Predictors of Job Performance." *Psychological Bulletin* 96, no. 1: 72–98.

Kluemper, Donald H., Benjamin D. McLarty, Terrence R. Bishop, and Anindita Sen. 2015. "Interviewee Selection Test and Evaluator Assessments of General Mental Ability, Emotional Intelligence and Extraversion: Relationships with Structured Behavioral and Situational Interview Performance." *Journal of Business Psychology* 30, no. 3: 543–63.

König, Cornelius J., Ute-Christine Klehe, Matthias Berchtold, and Martin Kleinmann. 2010. "Reasons for Being Selective When Choosing Personnel Selection Procedures." *International Journal of Selection & Assessment* 18, no. 1: 17–27.

Myers, David G. 2002. *Intuition: Its Powers and Perils.* New Haven, CT: Yale University Press.

Terpstra, David E., and Wanthanee Limpaphayom. 2012. "Using Evidence-Based Human Resource Practices for Global Competitiveness." *International Journal of Business and Management* 7, no. 12: 107–13.

Thomas, Steven L., and Steve Vaught. 2001. "The Write Stuff: What the Evidence Says About Using Handwriting Analysis in Hiring." *SAM Advanced Management Journal* 66, no. 4: 31–35.

Weak, Emily. 2014. "What Candidates Want: How to Practice Compassionate Hiring." *Library Leadership & Management* 28, no. 4: 1–4.

CHAPTER 5

Oversight and Administration of Reference Services

NO MATTER HOW IMPRESSIVE the library's resources, or how accomplished the library staff, it would be virtually impossible to provide reference services at a high level in any library without effective supervision and leadership. This chapter will cover several important aspects of reference administration. First is a discussion of the nature of reference services supervision, with particular attention to the broad roles and unusual organizational status of the position. Next are tips on developing a vision of reference services, and communicating this vision to all stakeholders. Taking responsibility for even a portion of the library budget can be a daunting hurdle for many librarians, but this chapter will discuss the level of knowledge necessary to take some of the mystery and intimidation away from library finances. Finally, an explanation of the fundamentals of library assessment will provide a solid foundation for practical evaluation of the performance of a reference services operation.

⊚ Reference Services and the Middle Manager

Barring the one-person operation or libraries with only a few employees, the individual charged with overseeing reference services in most libraries occupies an amorphous area of administration that is often called middle management. The position may have various titles, such as supervisor, coordinator, head of reference, or team leader. For the sake of continuity, "reference supervisor" will be used in this chapter. Whatever the title, however, persons accepting accountability for reference must respond to the dual challenges of upholding the priorities of their organization while maintaining high standards of reference service. They must be involved in the details of day-to-day operations, yet these day-to-day activities must always be guided toward fulfillment of the library's broader objectives.

Maintaining an effective balance among the conflicting needs and priorities of reference services can be a formidable task for any reference supervisor. The situation may be further complicated by confusion over the role and authority structure for the position. For example, the person in charge of reference is often not part of the highest level of library leadership. As such, the reference supervisor may not have a voice in major decisions of policy and strategy, yet bears considerable accountability for the performance of this critical area of library operations. Moreover, the reference supervisor may be responsible for coordinating coverage of the reference desk, yet have no real authority over the reference librarians. The reference supervisor may also be answerable for establishing reference policies and guiding staff development, yet some (or all) of the reference staff may not report directly to the reference supervisor.

The reference supervisor position need not, however, be an ineffective or powerless one. On the contrary, skillful guidance of reference services is indispensable in the current environment of constant change in our libraries. Supervision of reference services may, in fact, represent the first step into library administration and management for many librarians. The experience is valuable precisely because there is ambiguity in the role and hierarchical status of the position. It forces the novice supervisor to accomplish objectives without depending on rank and direct authority—skills that become increasingly important the higher a person climbs in any organization. It is also a good way for many library staff and librarians to test the waters of administration. Not everyone is a good fit for a supervisory role, and the hands-on aspects of reference services supervision can provide a relatively low-risk trial run.

The Roles of the Reference Supervisor

Exactly what, then, should be expected of the reference supervisor? How many kinds of roles and responsibilities are appropriate to this position? The answers to these questions will vary according to the size, mission, and organization structure of the specific library. The responsibilities of a reference supervisor in a public library are different from those in an academic library, while responsibilities within a private corporate library might seem to have little in common with either of the others. Nonetheless, even in this time of sweeping changes in librarianship, there are a few roles common to nearly every reference supervisor. Below is a brief description of some of these roles, many of which will be covered in more detail later in this or in other chapters:

- *Team leader: the train must always be guided by a good engineer.* Perhaps in a small library it is the library director, while in a major research library it may be someone at the level of a department head, but someone needs to organize the many people and activities required to run a reference services operation. This is true even when, as is often the case, the supervisor is not actually the person who creates the rules and policies. The reference supervisor must create a cohesive, effective group, juggling the need for communication, conflict resolution, strong standards, counseling, training, and much more. At the same time, this is not a job that can be effectively managed through authoritarian means. Dealing effectively with the public requires a reference staff that is happy and motivated, and such a staff must be nurtured using thoughtful persuasion and equitable negotiation rather than harsher methods.

- *Project manager: someone has to keep the trains up and running.* Keeping a library relevant, effective, and attractive to its users takes persistent tinkering with existing systems, and a constant drive to discover new ways to improve services. Finding the time, talent, funding, and political will to make the necessary changes can be difficult even in the best circumstances. The reference supervisor must be able to design projects and activities to improve the library and its reference services in a consequential way, despite ever-present financial and practical constraints.

- *Planner: someone needs to keep the trains running on time.* Producing a schedule for reference services may require a careful examination of traffic and usage patterns, and it demands considerable finesse to negotiate staffing at the hours needed rather than at the hours staff would like to work. In other cases, the challenge may be scheduling the right people at the right time. Some library staff, for example, may be better able to work during busy hours serving multiple demands, while others have the self-discipline to complete in-depth tasks during slow times. This staffing challenge is in addition to planning around holidays, vacations, illnesses, and family responsibilities. The diplomatic skills the supervisor brings to these seemingly trivial concerns can have powerful effects on the productivity and morale of the reference staff.

- *Evaluator: someone has to keep an eye on the dashboard lights.* There are many moving parts in reference services, and someone needs to determine what is working (and what is not), how well it is working, and how fast it is working. Perhaps even more important is determining what you actually mean by something "working." What benchmarks and metrics are the most valid? What goals are reasonable and accomplishable? How do you measure your reference collection's effectiveness? How do you measure the effectiveness of reference transactions? There is as much art as science in finding meaningful answers to these questions.

- *Collaborator: someone else needs to help out on the train.* Reference services are not an island. Done well, libraries are the heart of their campuses and communities—and, done well, reference services are the heart of the library. All of the collections, all of the technical services, all of the administration, and all of the physical space in the library is attached to its users through reference services. The more knowledgeable the reference staff is about all aspects of the library, the more adeptly they can lead library users to the best the library has to offer. The better the relationship of reference services to library users and to the community as a whole, the better the channels of communication. The library is not just stuff; it is a system of interactions and relationships. Nowhere is this more apparent than in reference services. The role of collaboration and outreach is discussed in greater detail in chapter 6.

With such a list of possible roles, how does the aspiring reference supervisor know which of these many responsibilities are a part of the expectations for a specific position? First, it is critical to read job descriptions and postings carefully, and to ask questions before accepting a job offer. It is unquestionably worth the effort to discuss and negotiate terms so that everyone is working from the same set of expectations. If you are already employed as a reference supervisor but are unclear about your responsibilities and level of authority, it is not too late to speak to your superiors to get a clearer understanding. It is sometimes considered unseemly to renegotiate your responsibilities after you have accepted a position, but a good track record of positive accomplishments may convince your superiors that you are deserving of an exception. It is always worth asking, if only for the sake of clarification.

Putting Priorities in Balance

With reference supervision potentially covering so many different responsibilities in so many areas, simply deciding where to begin can be intimidating. In searching for a starting point, though, there is probably no management principal more fundamental to success than this: *maintain awareness of the interrelationships of all administrative and managerial functions*. Business author Victor Lipman (2014: n.p.) states, "Like so much in life, successful management involves balance—juggling multiple priorities, usually with too much to do in too little time. Tilt too much in any one direction and the managerial ship sails easily off course." The daily life of a reference services supervisor may be seen, in fact, as a series of attempts to balance competing demands in almost every area.

The reference supervisor must, for example, balance and negotiate the needs of many stakeholders. Maybe the reference staff would like to be home with their families and friends on the weekends and evenings, whereas library users would like to see reference hours extended. Perhaps library administrators need to cut costs, while staff would like to see wage increases and library users are demanding increased access to expensive online resources. It is often the reference supervisor who stands at the crossroads of these differing viewpoints, seeking practical solutions through relationship building and consistent attention to feedback from a variety of sources.

Another critical issue is balancing the divergent demands of management and leadership. Søren Jagd explains the distinction between the two as follows:

> Leadership is in many ways similar to management. Leadership and management both involve influence, entail working with people, and are concerned with goal accomplishment. Nevertheless, the functions of leadership may also be seen as quite different from management. While management produces order and consistency, leadership produces change and movement. (2009: 988)

Some leadership experts suggest a mutual exclusivity between leadership and management. A reference supervisor must, according to this line of reasoning, choose to be either a leader (a person of vision who creates teams of followers) or a manager (a foot soldier who carries out orders from above). In a library environment, however, it is more productive to view these as separate but indispensable elements of the same role. There must be balance between carrying out the prevailing policies and objectives established by library administration on the one hand, and creating effective and exciting innovations on the other. Finding the balance point between the reliable and the adventurous, and between comfortable traditions and refreshing changes, is essential. Finding this hypothetical sweet spot is one of the most valuable accomplishments of reference supervision.

The sections that follow are designed to help reference supervisors find that center of balance in their own reference operations.

⑥ A Vision for Reference Services

Like most employed people, librarians spend much of their time and energy on day-to-day issues that crop up in their immediate areas of concern. For example, a reference librarian may be (justifiably) focused on answering questions from library users and scrutinizing daily reference staffing schedules. This is certainly not a bad thing—performing the basic functions of your job to the best of your ability is its own justification. Effective leadership, however, demands that individuals overseeing reference services sometimes raise their gaze from the grindstone to take a broader view. An epigram often loosely attributed as a Japanese proverb goes, "Vision without action is a daydream. Action without vision is a nightmare."

To return to our theme of balance, the successful supervisor must balance the need for immediate and tangible action with the need to tie actions to strategic goals and objectives in a coherent vision of reference services. A thoughtful, compelling vision for reference services is one powerful means of doing exactly this.

Creating a Vision

Leadership and management literature is awash in theories and arguments regarding the optimal approach to developing an organizational vision. Some are exhaustive exercises encompassing large committees of organizational leaders working for many months (or even years) and resulting in comprehensive documents running to hundreds of pages. Some of these documents bring about real organizational change, and some are slipped into drawers and promptly forgotten.

For the purposes of running a good reference services operation, however, a more humble approach should fulfill the need. A reference vision, in this instance, is nothing more than a solid idea of what you believe reference services should look like in your library over the next few years. It is also a good idea to incorporate a basic plan for making this happen, including workable timelines. Below are some of the specific steps you might take to create a fully formed vision of reference services:

- *Align with the institutional vision.* Most libraries have already created institutional vision statements. These statements go by a variety of terms: vision or mission statements, strategic plans, or objectives; in educational libraries, the vision may be described in terms of outcomes or competencies. It is important to locate your organization's vision statement, and incorporate its goals and priorities into those being created for reference services. If you cannot find a vision statement, you should speak to your superiors, and perhaps even interview them at some length to completely understand their vision of the library and its operations.
- *Align with the input of stakeholders.* You can ensure that you develop an inclusive vision by seeking and incorporating input from people representing all viewpoints on reference services. Speak to library users, staff, and administrators, and to relevant groups and leaders in your community. This does not necessarily require a formal research process—casual interviews or a brief survey should be adequate in most cases. Do not stop, however, until you are confident you have a solid understanding of the needs and preferences of all concerned.

- *Discover your organizational history.* Find out about past attempts to do the kinds of things you are planning to do. Find out why previous attempts failed, and use this knowledge to create a better approach for your current plans.
- *Consider a quick SWOT analysis of your reference services.* A SWOT analysis is an examination of the **S**trengths, **W**eaknesses, **O**pportunities, and **T**hreats you perceive for your reference operation. Again, this need not be an arduous process—just take a few minutes to consider the environment you face from the current time through the next few years. Take a few notes, and use this information to inform your vision for reference services. This brief exercise will help you to focus on prospects for improvement, while remaining watchful for signs of potential problems.
- *Create the vision.* Once you have given due consideration to all of the above, you should be ready to translate this information into a solid, detailed picture of the current condition of your reference services, and a vision for what your operation could become over the next few years. Make your vision aspirational (be bold enough to dream of truly top-notch, innovative reference services) but realistic (recognize and plan for the challenges and limitations you might face). Show your vision statement to those you trust and ask for honest, constructive feedback, then incorporate the best of those comments into the final version.
- *Make it real.* Now that you know where you want to go with reference services, you need to develop a plan to get there. Think realistically about moving toward your goals. If you wish to improve staff performance, you might create a plan of developmental training activities. If you wish to improve the reference collection, discuss funding with your superiors. With a clear idea of your goals and persistent work in that direction, you can achieve significant results over a surprisingly short period.
- *Communicate your vision.* It is critical to make sure that everyone is aware of your vision for reference services, and that you develop and maintain momentum. Present your plan publicly, and distribute it widely. If you have incorporated the viewpoints of all stakeholders as discussed previously, complaints and resistance should be minimal, but incorporate feedback wherever possible. Most importantly, make certain that everyone understands your objectives and the reasoning behind them.
- *Launch your program!* It is important to put your plan into action and then to maintain it through constant upkeep and attention. Monitor your progress in the most objective terms possible, and communicate the results to stakeholders consistently to keep your vision present and fresh in everyone's mind. Establish predetermined points in time to perform a complete review of the results, and do not be afraid to make revisions to keep your program on track.

The steps outlined above should help you create a compelling vision for a reference services operation, but they are certainly not set in stone. There are as many different approaches to finding and creating a vision as there are visions—each unique and separate. This is as it should be. However you approach the creation of a reference services vision, though, it should incorporate the following qualities:

- The vision must be significant, memorable, and moving
- The language should be simple, clear, and comprehensible
- The message must be understood by all, and enjoy the approval of most
- Results should be verifiable in the most objective way possible

Benefits of a Strong Vision for Reference Services

At this point some readers might question whether such a process is, after all, really worth the trouble. To the cynical, there might seem little point trying to develop a sense of direction for reference services when many of the big decisions are made several levels above the reference supervisor. Some librarians (and occasionally whole libraries) are, moreover, set in their ways, and instituting change may turn out to be an unpopular or simply unrealistic goal. While true enough, these objections may be beside the point. To begin, it is likely that the supervisor can build such resistance into the plan. Knowing you will not gain support for sweeping change from your colleagues could lead to negotiating for changes that are more incremental. Start small, show success, and you should be able to gradually increase the number of people who will back your efforts.

A similar approach may hold for resistant or dismissive superiors. Even in organizations in which power is held tightly at the top, virtually every leader seeks ways to improve results and achieve organizational goals. If you have tied your goals to the objectives of your organization, it is hard to imagine a situation in which library administration would refuse, if not support you actively, at least to give you some leeway to try out your ideas. Remember also that the difficulties you face in establishing a vision for reference services must be balanced against the many benefits. A good vision statement:

- Provides a sense of direction for reference services
- Offers a clear yardstick of accomplishments and progress
- Improves the supervisor's ability to allocate time and resources appropriately
- Removes extraneous distractions and avoids wasting time on outdated priorities
- Allows the supervisor to make necessary changes before things reach a crisis point
- Makes for more effective staff development and succession planning
- Makes a statement about your values to your staff, to library administrators, and to your community

It is important to remember these many benefits, and equally important to remind others of them. This is the final step in bringing your ideas to fruition—staying the course. After a first acceptance, many new programs or ideas run their course and die a quiet death. To remain lively, your vision for reference services must, like a rosebush, be nurtured carefully, pruned and fed, protected from predators, and sheltered during the harsh seasons. It will require an ongoing commitment to maintain and improve the original vision, or eventually, when the time is right, to uproot and supplant this vision with a new one.

⌖ Budgets, Funding, and Cost Control

Budget cuts and funding shortfalls have become a way of life for most librarians, regardless of library type or location. There is no question that this situation has created impediments to providing quality reference services (Saunders, 2013). When staffing levels fall, that increases the workload for the remaining staff. When salary and benefits stagnate or lose ground to the cost of living, motivation is affected, and turnovers increase. Furthermore, the possibility of lost positions and potential layoffs increases stress levels.

The impact of these and other forms of fallout from shrinking budgets may vary by library, but hard economic realities loom large over almost every library function and activity. It is unfortunate that the financial challenges faced by libraries are actually exacerbated by the lack of training in budget management most librarians receive (or are willing to receive) in their library science programs. According to the American Library Association, on its "Budgeting & Finance" web page (2015), "Librarians share a love of words, but sometimes the most important tasks involve crunching the numbers."

In truth, there is no reason to fear financial planning for reference services. Managing the budget for even the most involved reference operation is a straightforward task, less complicated than the personal finances of most households. Taking responsibility for the reference services budget can, in fact, be a surprisingly rewarding experience, even in times of financial difficulty. Going through the budgeting process provides a chance to begin from scratch and review all of the assumptions that underlie reference services in your library. This is the time when "we've always done it that way" is simply not an adequate response (if it ever is), and every decision can be examined for opportunities to improve the efficiency and quality of reference services (Nicholas et al., 2010). Reviewing the reference services budget means leaving no stone unturned, including hours of operation, staffing, services, and anything else that falls under the broadest definition of reference services. Everything can be re-examined later, so the supervisor should be bold in considering every conceivable financial variable during the first pass.

Dealing with the reference budget is normally a relatively low-stress task. For better or worse, the reference supervisor rarely holds sole (or even primary) accountability for the actual reference budget. The big money decisions are made by the major players—the dean and department heads in an academic library, the city or county council and library directors in a public library, and so forth. As a middle manager, the reference supervisor may have a lesser or greater voice in the budget process, but real control resides elsewhere. This is yet another instance in which reference supervision provides a good first step on the path to greater administrative responsibilities: supervisors should have a solid understanding of what is being spent and why, but they can take comfort in the knowledge that they will not be dealing with finances unaided.

Though reference supervisors do not normally hold exclusive responsibility for the budgeting process, they should nonetheless take the most active role possible. This means finding out who actually does control the budget, and understanding their priorities and strategies. It means opening clear channels of communication and mutual cooperation with library administrators and other departments. The creation of an effective library budget is an interactive process, and the degree to which the reference supervisor develops collegial alliances may help to determine the overall standing of reference services in the library, and the ability of reference services to obtain the support and funding needed to reach key objectives.

The Library Budget

A sample library budget is shown in table 5.1. This is a rough example, created with imaginary figures and a broad sample of generic items you might expect to see in an annual budget for almost any type of library. This particular example shows only operational expenditures—the costs involved in actually running the library on a day-to-day basis. A full budget would also include capital expenditures, which are long-term major purchases such as property, buildings, and expensive equipment. Capital expenditures are well be-

Table 5.1.   Sample Library Budget

ITEM DESCRIPTION	2015–2016	2014–2015	2013–2014
Personnel	**3,450,000**	**3,260,209**	**2,925,939**
Librarians	1,830,000	1,729,328	1,552,020
Staff	1,256,000	1,186,905	1,065,211
Student assistants	364,000	343,976	308,708
Facility costs	**625,000**	**590,617**	**530,061**
Telecommunications	133,000	125,683	112,797
Utilities	178,000	168,208	150,961
Maintenance	314,000	296,726	266,303
Supplies	**123,000**	**116,234**	**104,316**
Office and administrative	54,000	51,029	45,797
Office computers and copiers	48,000	45,360	40,709
Furniture and shelving	21,000	19,845	17,810
Systems (software and hardware)	**800,000**	**755,991**	**678,479**
Technology and audio/visual	514,000	485,724	435,923
Software	286,000	270,267	242,556
Collections and acquisitions	**2,950,000**	**2,787,715**	**2,501,889**
Databases and consortium fees	2,027,600	1,916,058	1,719,604
Books	830,000	784,340	703,921
Serials	72,000	68,039	61,063
DVDs/CDs	2,400	2,268	2,035
Other	18,000	17,010	15,266
Miscellaneous operating costs	**123,000**	**116,234**	**104,316**
Travel and development	56,000	52,919	47,493
Institutional memberships	45,000	42,524	38,164
Events and marketing	24,000	20,791	18,659
TOTAL BUDGET	**$8,071,000**	**$7,627,000**	**$6,845,000**

yond the scope of the reference supervisor's responsibilities. The sample budget shown also excludes revenues and income—the amount of money the library takes in.

The primary sources of library funding—community or state tax revenues, campus funding plans, and major grants or endowments—are also outside the immediate control of the reference supervisor. This should not be taken to imply that a reference supervisor should not be aware of broader fiscal issues. All responsible library employees, and especially those filling a supervisory role, should understand how their institutions are funded, and how these funds are being spent. For the supervisor in a library environment, though, budgeting for expenses and controlling costs will normally be the primary financial focus.

In reviewing the operational expenditures in table 5.1, you might note that there is no specific mention of reference services. Reference-related expenses are part of these budget items, however, and it is important that the reference supervisor understand how budget changes can affect reference operations. Personnel costs are, for example, normally the largest expense for a library, even at a time when the costs of print and electronic research materials are skyrocketing. Understanding the part reference services play in these expenses is crucial to making the best use of available assets. Consider how each of the major areas of operational expenses interacts with reference services:

- *Personnel.* This major expense will be the first one scrutinized in difficult fiscal times. The reference supervisor should be prepared to defend staffing levels in the most objective, rational manner possible. Show, for example, that reference staffing has adjusted fluidly to changes in reference traffic and the number of transactions completed. It may be effective to show that you have used student assistants or library interns to fill staffing gaps efficiently. You might also present evidence that you have saved funds by limiting turnover among your highly qualified staff.
- *Facility costs.* Running a facility the size and complexity of most libraries is a difficult and expensive undertaking. It is unlikely that reference services will be called on to repair plumbing or install a new roof, but there are many ways reference services and the facilities budget interrelate. Consider, for instance, that an expansion of reference hours may incur additional utility costs. Alternatively, improvements in the library's telecommunications contract may mean better telephone and texting service for reference patrons. Examine your current needs. Perhaps your reference operation required two separate telephone lines in the past, but now you could do with one. Dropping your service to one line may free up funds for other needs, and your willingness to contribute to the fiscal well-being of the library as a whole will not go unnoticed.
- *Supplies.* Supplies are generally a small part of the library budget, and include such commonplace items as printer paper, office supplies, cleaning supplies, and supplies for events and activities. It is sometimes hard to see how frugality in the distribution of paper clips can affect the overall fiscal well-being of a library, but often the smallest items send the strongest message. When you ask staff members to re-use paper clips and save rubber bands, for example, you communicate in clear terms that even little things count. Every paper clip, every sheet of paper, every stain on the carpet, and every reference transaction counts—and it all affects the efficiency of reference services as a unit.
- *Systems.* In the current technological environment, computer systems are the frame on which the entire library hangs. Libraries and library consortiums make enormous investments of time and money locating the best systems for library needs, and finding the funds to pay for them. So important has this area become that it is usually placed under the control of computer specialists rather than librarians, but every librarian should be intimately aware of the systems and software being used by the library, along with any alternatives that may be available. The reference supervisor should understand how new systems might affect the usability of major services such as catalogs and search systems, as well as minor functions like room reservations and scheduling.
- *Collections and acquisitions.* Management of the reference collection, both print and electronic, is a critical concern for any library. Even in an era when the Internet

promises (falsely) to provide every pertinent piece of information available, the library must provide access to carefully selected, reliable, accurate, up-to-date information. In truth, the uneven quality of content on the Internet makes it more important than ever for the library remain a trustworthy and unbiased source of knowledge. The topic of reference collection development is discussed in more detail in chapter 2, but the budgetary challenge of keeping the reference collection current is an important issue unto itself. For decades, libraries have suffered a staggering rate of inflation for journals, databases, and high-quality reference books—at the same time that library budgets are shrinking relentlessly. As a result, reference supervisors must optimize every dollar spent on the reference collection.

- *Other expenses*—clinging to the edges of every library budget are the miscellaneous expenses. None of them are important enough to merit a separate section of the budget, yet each provides enough value to the operation of the library that they cannot be discarded. In the sample budget shown in table 5.1, miscellaneous expenses comprise general travel expenses, the cost of staff development, and funds for marketing and events. In other libraries, this might also include small awards or contributions to community causes, staff parties, or any of a number of small, valid expenditures that don't fit existing classifications. The fact that these expenses are small should not, however, exclude them from careful scrutiny. Needless travel, extravagant foods and beverages for meetings, and a thousand other seemingly inconsequential indulgences can chew away at budgets that are, in all other respects, carefully constrained.

This sample budget may be much simpler than many real library budgets, but more detailed than others. Whatever form the budget takes in your library, though, it is always in your interest to examine it thoroughly. Nothing will tell you more about the priorities of your organization than a review of the decisions made about money.

LIBRARY BUDGET CUTS ARE NOT A NEW PHENOMENON

When we assign monetary resources, we vote on our future in a highly practical, meaningful way, and the future may well judge us on how these decisions were made. Novotny (2010) writes that the Chicago Public Library, facing severe budget cuts during the Great Depression in the 1930s, chose to cut back on materials and subscriptions rather than sacrifice people. The libraries retained almost all of their employees (though on a reduced pay scale) and maintained standard hours of operation. These decisions were likely made to help avoid making local unemployment worse. During these difficult years, people flocked to the public libraries in Chicago. They came to seek advice and insight for dealing with the crushing problems they faced every day, or they came to find an escape from these same problems—but they came. When the lack of new materials and resources began to affect circulation, the libraries turned to the community for donations and support. In other words, all of the budget-related issues came down to the relationship of the library to its employees and its community. It may be helpful to remember this lesson from the past—viewing the library budget as, among other things, a roadmap for achieving and maintaining the library's many valuable relationships.

The Reference Services Budget

The priorities implied by the main library budget mean little, however, if they do not translate into actionable programs for every area of the library. For this reason, many areas of the library have their own budgets. Acquisitions and collections may, for instance, be summarized as a single aggregated item in the main library budget, but almost certainly there will also be a more detailed budget showing how the collections budget will be spent. Table 5.2 gives an example of such a separate budget for a hypothetical reference operation. This sample budget is also highly generalized, and the actual budget for reference services in any specific library may vary widely from this model. The major classifications shown are, nonetheless, worth considering for any reference operation.

In this sample there are four major classifications: personnel, supplies, resources, and technology. Depending on the administrative model for a particular library, the reference supervisor may be asked to take responsibility for all of these areas, or none. Even if not specifically called upon to control these budget lines, however, supervisors should understand the resources at their disposal and manage them responsibly.

In the sample budget shown in table 5.2, for example, the cost of reference librarians is classified in its entirety as a reference expense. This is rarely the case in most libraries—reference librarians perform many functions in administration and instruction, and their duties normally range over too many departments and areas to be borne by reference services alone. Even if all of the hours worked by reference librarians are not charged directly to reference, though, the reference supervisor will certainly be called upon to account for

Table 5.2.   Sample Reference Services Budget

ITEM DESCRIPTION	COST ($)
Personnel	**791,000**
Reference librarians	700,000
Reference staff	56,000
Reference student assistants	35,000
Supplies	**2,450**
Tissues, sanitizer, etc.	200
Pens, pencils, paper clips	150
Printer paper, toner	2,100
Resources	**25,000**
Books	20,000
Subscriptions	5,000
Technology	**20,600**
Research guide system	12,000
Miscellaneous software	8,000
Reference computers maintenance	600
TOTAL BUDGET	**839,050**

the use of librarian time. Staff and student assistants assigned specifically to reference are normally charged entirely to reference services. The time and talents of all reference personnel should be used wisely, tracked diligently, and justified completely.

However the fiscal responsibilities for reference services are distributed, the most important consideration for the reference supervisor is gaining a clear understanding of the resources under the control of reference services: which resources are involved, what quantities have been allotted, and what quantities will be needed. The use of all resources should be traced and documented thoroughly, so the supervisor is prepared to answer questions about what has become of them. This is a crucial responsibility for supervisors—even if this information has not been required or requested in the past, situations can shift suddenly, and in some cases retroactively. The prudent supervisor will remain vigilant and prepare for all eventualities.

Cost Control

Once a budget has been created and agreed upon by the relevant parties, it must become a real framework for spending. This is a critical standard for supervisor performance. By demonstrating that you have been responsible with the funding you receive currently, you give your superiors reason to have confidence that you will use future allotments efficiently to reach desired objectives. By showing that you are a trustworthy steward of organizational resources, you may also substantially affect the way in which library administrators view your existing supervisory skills, and your potential to move into greater responsibility in the future.

Effective control of resources is a skill that takes time and experience to master, but what follows are some practical tips to start you in the right direction:

- *Prioritize carefully.* Use institutional mission statements, budgets, and initiatives to help create priorities and goals for reference services. In this way you are helping to reach organizational goals as you fulfill goals in your own areas of responsibility.
- *Make evidence-based decisions.* It is important to base decisions, even the day-to-day sort, on reliable, objective information. Collecting and examining hourly reference traffic, for example, is an excellent method for determining the distribution of reference desk coverage. Viewing data collected over a period of time will make you aware of trends, which will help to overcome short-term thinking.
- *Be aware of organizational accounting practices.* Work to develop at least a general understanding of how your library handles the budget process, fiscal periods, and the practical rules of accounting. Learning to comply with complicated rules and shifting due dates for record keeping, funding requests, and other accounting requirements can be challenging, but the effort pays ample dividends in good relations with those who control the organization's purse strings.
- *Understand "the system."* Take an active role in discovering and incorporating the unspoken rules of your organization's budget process. In some organizations, for example, using less than the allotted funding for a given fiscal year simply results in less funding in future budgets. In other cases, it is expected that your funding requests are inflated to allow some room for negotiation. If you request the amount you really need, some administrators will assume you can live with 10 percent less, actually allotting 20 percent less to make you stretch your resources. This is not to

suggest that you should make proposals dishonestly or unethically, but do understand how your administrators view such practices, and take this into account as you plan.

A little forethought and preparation before the budget planning process begins can help supervisors handle reference assets in a prudent manner, and can eliminate worry and misunderstandings about the efficiency of reference operations. The modest output of time required can yield significant returns in trust, confidence, and stability. Budget planning is also an excellent opportunity to communicate openly with administrators about fiscal needs, both in the present and the future. All reference supervisors should accept the challenge of learning at least the fundamentals of library budgeting.

Assessing Reference Services

One of the best ways to show that reference operations are working efficiently and making good use of resources is a carefully considered program of assessment. Assessment is among the most important, and in some ways the most difficult, of the many responsibilities of the reference supervisor. All of the hard work invested in providing the best reference services operation can go wrong if there is not an effective assessment program in place to confirm that your reference operations are doing what you think they are.

Unfortunately, librarians often do not, as a group, show great enthusiasm for undertaking objective evaluations of the services they provide. As Joseph R. Matthews (2007: 4) points out, "Traditionally, librarians have relied on instincts and experience to make decisions." Matthews goes on to suggest that libraries develop what he calls a "culture of assessment," a "culture of evidence," and a "culture of curiosity." Done properly, assessment of reference services can fulfill many useful functions, and can provide a number of practical benefits, including:

- *Tracking and improving performance*—gathering information about the effectiveness of reference activities and the usefulness of reference resources to identify strengths and weaknesses
- *Planning*—using solid evidence to identify needs and objectives in such areas as training, staffing, policy, and procedure
- *Making management decisions*—determining whether specific services should be reduced or increased, or whether they should be kept at all
- *Allocating resources*—using data-driven decision making to guide assets in ways that will increase the effectiveness of successful programs, or correct issues in problem areas

Developing an Assessment Plan

The advantages of assessment can be obtained only when assessment procedures are designed thoughtfully and carried out properly. Maintaining endless counts of random activities and sporadically distributing offhand questionnaires may produce some useful, if limited, information, but a systematic, consistent program of assessment will yield the greatest benefits. This is not to say, however, that assessment needs to be an overly complicated ordeal involving arcane statistical analysis or the endless collection of obscure data.

Assessment, for the purposes of the reference supervisor, has practical objectives that can be accomplished through relatively simple, straightforward methods. Keep in mind that you are just trying to determine whether reference services are working effectively. The more complex aspects of assessment are generally not relevant to the needs of reference services, though some academic libraries or large public libraries may adopt a more ambitious approach. In such cases, however, an academic specialist or assessment professional would normally provide guidance.

The first step in developing an assessment plan is entirely obvious, and yet it can be surprisingly thorny in practice: deciding what you want to assess, and why. This requires carefully identifying those measurable variables that represent the condition or performance of reference services. It may be something as simple as determining the number of reference transactions completed over a period of time, perhaps undertaken to fulfill mandatory institutional reporting requirements. At the other end of the continuum, the reference supervisor may be called on to create a detailed forecast of all reference operations for the next five to ten years, taking a wide range of influencing factors into consideration. Assessment can be time-consuming, labor-intensive, and sometimes costly, so it is critical to be clear on the rationale and objectives that underlie your assessment plan.

In almost all cases, the best foundation on which to build assessment goals are the goals of the organization. By knowing how your library, university, or organization defines success, you can incorporate its values into all aspects of reference operations. Having done so, you can then plan assessments to provide evidence of the reference contribution to institutional goals. If, for example, the primary challenge facing your library is reducing costs in response to budget cuts, then your assessments may focus on tracking reference expenditures, including variable costs such as staffing hours and supplies. By showing that you have consistently controlled and reduced expenses for reference operations, you show that you have contributed effectively to reaching the library's goals.

Cost controls do not work in isolation, though, and this is another important aspect of assessment planning. Controlling reference expenses is only a valid accomplishment if, in doing so, you have continued to maintain consistent standards across all reference services. This must be a central consideration in planning reference assessment: however many variables are isolated in specific evaluations and surveys, the individual outcomes must be viewed as a unified whole. It should be clear that the end result of a carefully planned reference assessment program should be a complete, accurate portrait of the state of reference services—diversified but coherent, objective yet insightful.

Types of Data

There are many kinds of data and information that can be collected as part of the reference services assessment process. Choosing the appropriate type of data should be a relatively straightforward process if you base your assessment plan on the organization's goals, as described above. Even with this good beginning, however, there are so many alternatives available that it becomes easy to stray from your original assessment goals. First, for example, you will have to decide between quantitative and qualitative data. The two types of data tell us fundamentally different things. Quantitative data is a measurement of the quantity or amount of something. It could refer to the number of reference questions received, or how many reams of paper were used at the reference printer. It would not, however, tell you how difficult the reference questions were, or whether the print quality was consistently high. That kind of knowledge would derive from qualitative data, which relates to the quality of a variable—assessing how good something is, or how much users like it. Quantitative assessment methods are often preferred by managers and administrators, because they usually relay forthright numerical information. On the other hand, qualitative data may provide a more nuanced view of characteristics that numbers alone can't describe. There are many ways to describe types of data; a very rough description of the general types you might collect for assessment of reference services are listed here:

- *Frequency.* Frequency data refers to information about a quantity of something (how many pencils have we used?) or the number of times something happens (how many people have visited the reference desk in person?) over a designated amount of time. Frequency data is clearly quantitative, and is the simplest form of assessment. But it is usually most helpful when combined with other types of information. Perhaps the supervisor examines the number of transactions per hour, but then also examines staffing per hour; both data sets need to be classified by day of the week (are Mondays busier than Thursdays?) or by the difficulty of the questions (simple directional questions, or complicated research problems?).
- *Perception.* Gathering data about user perceptions can be quite helpful. This information can tell how your users regard your services, staff, resources, and the organization as a whole. Are library patrons aware of all your services? Perhaps they know there is a reference desk, but do not know you also answer questions online. Are they satisfied with the service they have received? Was their problem solved? Were they treated respectfully and professionally? Are they comfortable asking questions, or is the placement of your reference staff too public for confidential questions? Alternatively, how does your staff feel about their ability to help library users given the resources the library offers? All of these questions are central to the success of reference services, yet obtaining valid answers can be difficult without an intelligently designed assessment plan.
- *Outcome.* Outcome-based data is arguably the most important information the supervisor can possess, and it is usually the most difficult to obtain. Matthews notes, "The role, purpose, and value of academic library assessment must be anchored in an organization's purpose" (2007: 2). Matthews was speaking of academic libraries, but every organization, and every department within that organization, has objectives based on outcome. Ideally, these objectives are based on the mission and goals of the organization, but translating the organizational mission into the succinct, objective terms of an assessment instrument can be a demanding task. If it can be done, however, the results of the assessment will correspond to the success of the service or resource, and this is a powerful tool to present to your superiors as evidence of the quality of reference services, and of your work as a reference supervisor. If you can show that the outcome-based assessment instrument is even close to being accurate and valid, it will be a strong indicator of overall performance.

Data Collection and Analysis

Once you have decided on what to measure in your assessment, the next step is to choose or develop an instrument to do so. There are many choices available, and little consensus as to the best way to proceed. In his review of the history of reference assessment, Logan concludes, "After many decades of defining, discussing, and experimenting, a universally accepted method of assessment [still] does not exist" (2009: 230). It is likely that the chief reason for a lack of standardization in reference assessment methods is the diversity of needs they must fulfill. This is not such a bad thing, on the whole—it simply indicates that assessment can be designed to respond to specific situations in specialized ways. What follows is a brief review of some instruments types that are useful and popular for reference services assessment. Further research is strongly recommended before you decide on a specific method, or proceed with a specific instrument.

- *"Off-the-shelf" instruments.* A common approach to library assessment is to use a survey or system that has already been designed and, in some instances, tested and validated. The advantages are obvious: there is no need to develop a new instrument, and the results can be directly compared to those from other institutions. Without doubt the best known of these is LibQual+. Widely used and rigorously tested, this instrument was designed in a collaborative arrangement between Texas A&M University and the Association of Research Libraries (ARL). The primary disadvantage for reference services assessment is equally obvious: only a few of the items deal with reference services specifically. If your library is already using this instrument, however, it may yield at least some information about reference services. Fees are required for the use of LibQual+.
- *Observation.* The most basic method of assessing nearly any process is to simply go and look at it. It is an easy, useful way of assessing reference operations. Close, consistent observation should, of course, be a routine part of any supervisor's job, and there is always something to be learned from being present and attentive to your area of responsibility. There are pronounced limits to the usefulness of observation as an evaluative tool, however. First, personal observations are susceptible to the preconceptions and personal biases of the observer (Campbell and Swift, 2006). It is much easier to see what you think you will see than to notice evidence that contradicts your existing beliefs. Another problem arises from what is sometimes called the observation effect, which holds that people may behave differently when they are being observed (Alvero and Austin, 2004). It is possible to overcome observation effects by using unobtrusive observation methods such as hidden cameras or mystery shoppers, but the ethics of such methods are questionable and could damage the morale and motivation of the staff. Observation can yield some useful information, but it is a limited sample of behavior that should have no more than a supporting role in any comprehensive assessment plan.
- *Surveys.* Another common method of collecting information about reference services is the survey. If you want to know what patrons think of reference services in your library, you can just ask them. The survey may consist of only a few questions resulting from casual curiosity, or it could be an extensive collection of items drawn from a pilot study of many potential issues. It may be collected on slips of paper, or through an online survey system such as SurveyMonkey or TypeForm. As you develop and deliver your survey, though, keep in mind that the results will consist entirely of the perceptions of the respondents, and the data can only be as accurate as those perceptions. A survey can tell you if your users *believe* they received good service, or if they *believe* they were treated with respect, but you are trusting those users to set the standards for their responses. Another common risk with surveys is fatigue—in an age when surveys are handed out for every service, from grocery stores to government agencies to health care providers, many people are so weary of taking surveys they may answer thoughtlessly, or not at all. For this reason, show

respect for your patrons by keeping surveys short and to the point, and distribute them no more frequently than is really needed.

- *Focus groups and interviews.* While surveys provide the chance to ask your users questions, some issues require the give-and-take of a real conversation. In these instances, direct interaction may be the best solution, either individually in the form of interviews, or in small focus groups. This approach allows the interviewer to ask respondents to expand on their initial responses, or to ask follow-up questions to steer inquiries in a new direction. The interviewer can also observe revealing nuances in the reaction and behavior of interviewees. Interviews and focus groups are useful for gaining a deeper understanding of user perceptions and reactions. They allow users to describe their needs and desires in some detail, and to pass along new ideas. This comes at a cost, however. Interviews and focus groups are time-consuming to schedule and perform. Transcribing and analyzing results is labor-intensive, and providing incentives for participation can be expensive. This is not, therefore, an approach to be undertaken lightly, but it does provide a level of insight that might not be attainable by other means. It is important to ensure that such methods are used only to assess critical strategic aspects of reference services that cannot be evaluated by simpler alternatives.

- *Electronic data and analytics.* The use of online library tools and resources has exploded in recent years, and one of the greatest advantages of these systems is the wide range and depth of statistical data that can be easily accessed, examined, manipulated, and then presented in a pleasing, comprehensible manner. Content management systems (used to create online resources such as web pages and research guides) allow tracking of the number of times a resource is accessed, when it is accessed, and the sources from which it is accessed. Reference tracking systems such as Springshare's LibAnalytics allow staff to log transactions electronically, and the resulting data can be viewed in terms of any number of variables (time, frequency, type of question, etc.). Another powerful tool for monitoring and analyzing the performance of web resources is Google Analytics (www.google.com/analytics). This free service allows users to track site visits, page views, average time on site, and much more. The systems described here are only a few examples of the many forms of digital statistics now available in the current market—and the number and variety will certainly continue to increase. So impressive are the capabilities of these systems, in fact, that there is a risk of becoming intoxicated by the easy accessibility of so much data. As with all forms of assessment, take care to choose your data not simply because it is available, but because it is directly relevant to your assessment objectives.

- *Return on investment (ROI).* In recent decades, many public and academic organizations have taken to examining their worth in terms of the value returned over and above the resources invested. The ROI for reference services, for example, could be expressed in simplest terms as the following ratio:

$$\frac{\text{Perceived returns from reference services}}{\text{Perceived costs of reference services}}$$

In this example, costs could be estimated by adding labor hours, supplies used, utilities, and perhaps even a rough estimate of the cost of the physical space occupied by reference. Returns could be calculated by placing a value on reference services performed, such as a dollar value on reference transactions. The total value of the reference services provided would then be divided by the total cost of providing them. A result greater than 1 would be indicate a positive value, and a result less than 1 would indicate a negative value. This is a basic example of the approach, but the potential complexities are beyond the scope of the current work. It should be noted, however, that there is considerable controversy concerning the use of ROI for library assessment. Tracy Nectoux points out that currency does not change hands for library services, so there is no business transaction in any real sense. She goes on to suggest that this makes us "fundamentally ill-suited to think of ourselves as a business" (Berstler and Nectoux, 2013: 184). With this in mind, it may be advisable to discuss ROI methods with organizational administrators before proceeding. If library administrators do not place credence in this methodology, there is little point in investing the time and effort required.

Data Analysis

Once an assessment method has been chosen and the data collected, the next step is data analysis. This process can range in complexity from the simplest forms of observation to a detailed statistical analysis of all aspects of reference services. In larger libraries, there may be an assessment specialist, or even an assessment committee, that works with the reference supervisor to design a program in line with the library's standards. In other cases, the reference supervisor must undertake the process alone. Whatever the expectations of your library, a few points are universal. First, be an honest evaluator: seek the truth that can be revealed by your data. Reference assessment was initially developed to improve the quality of service, but in many cases it has been reduced to a tool used to "justify and preserve" the status quo (Logan, 2009: 230). Make sure you analyze and report your results exactly as they stand—it can be tempting to bend numbers to your own desires or agenda, but in the long run, an accurate report will be more valuable than a fictional one.

The second point is to not overwork or overthink your results. Remember the purpose of your assessment: focus on finding answers to the questions you set out to answer. Don't read more into your results than is there—if the number of reference transactions is down, for example, don't jump to conclusions about the cause. It might be the weather, or a change in classroom assignments, or it might be some problem with the delivery of services—but you won't know until you perform follow-up research to find out. Finally, remember that good assessment is not just a snapshot of a single moment. Assessment is not a single point; it is a line travelling through a number of data points collected at intervals over time. Avoid panic over a temporary downturn or giddiness over a short-term gain—wait for the bigger picture to emerge in long-term trends.

Using Results to Guide Improvements

When all the data has finally been gathered and analyzed, the task of assessment is still far from finished. The real work is just beginning, as the ultimate goal of assessment is using the results to generate positive changes in reference services. As Matthews (2007) notes, data is often gathered but not used, or gathered specifically to justify a decision that has already been made. This is a waste of the time and expense required to conduct a thorough assessment. If, for example, surveys indicate dissatisfaction with the professionalism or knowledge of the reference staff, there is a temptation to disregard or even

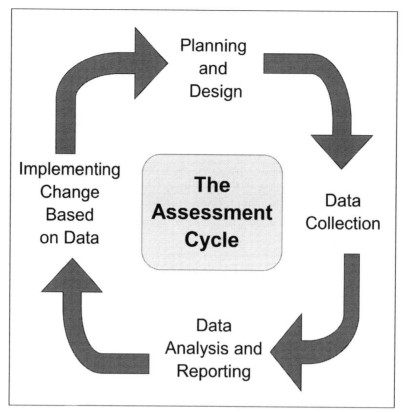

Figure 5.1.   The assessment cycle

hide such negative results. It is best to avoid such urges—acting on them would merely prolong the agony and embed problems more deeply. By dealing directly with negative assessment results, the benefits almost invariably outweigh the short-term problems. In the example above, taking an active approach in training and coaching the reference staff can alleviate problems, improve performance, and show your superiors that you can effect positive change.

Figure 5.1 illustrates the principle that assessment is a repeating cycle. The cycle begins with establishing clear goals and process planning, proceeds through data collection and analysis, and results in the implementation of improvements to reference services. As soon as this cycle completes, the process begins again. The supervisor continues to monitor the performance of reference services, perhaps by tracking data on an ongoing basis, or undertaking brief pilot studies to examine particular areas of concern. This may result in minor corrections or revisions. Then, at a time usually predetermined as part of assessment planning, the cycle begins again. The process of self-examination and renewal must proceed continuously to keep reference services fresh and relevant.

⦿ Key Points

Particularly at a time when reference services transform so frequently and dramatically, skilled leadership will be critical in creating innovative approaches to keep reference services useful well into the future. This chapter has provided a broad introduction to some of the most fundamental methods and principles used in the oversight of reference services.

- Effective leadership of reference services requires that the supervisor simultaneously responds to the needs of library users, reference staff, and library administrators.
- Reference services objectives are easier to achieve when the reference staff, reference supervisor, and library administrators have a mutual understanding as to what success should look like at reference.
- Financial planning and controlling costs for reference services can be intimidating for the uninitiated, but taking the time to learn the fundamentals of library budgeting can help to keep reference services running efficiently.
- Accurate assessment of reference services begins with a clear understanding of what is being assessed, and must be carried out using valid data collection methods appropriate to the objectives of the assessment.

The next chapter will discuss effective outreach through the marketing of reference services and development of beneficial collaborative partnerships.

References

Alvero, Alicia M., and John Austin. 2004. "The Effects of Conducting Behavioral Observations on the Behavior of the Observer." *Journal of Applied Behavioral Analysis* 37, no. 4: 457–68.

American Library Association. 2015. "Budgeting & Finance." http://www.ala.org/tools/atoz/librarybudgetfinance/budgetfinance.

Berstler, Andrea, and Tracy Nectoux. 2013. "Should Libraries Be Run Like Businesses?" *Reference & User Services Quarterly* 52, no. 3: 222–24.

Campbell, Constance E., and Cathy Owens Swift. 2006. "Attributional Comparisons across Biases and Leader-Member Exchange Status." *Journal of Managerial Issues* 18, no. 3: 393–408.

Jagd, Søren. 2009. "Leadership." In *Encyclopedia of Business in Today's World*, edited by Charles Wankel, 988–89. Los Angeles: Sage Publications.

Lipman, Victor, 2014. "6 Reasons Effective Management Requires Balance." *Forbes*, February 21. http://www.forbes.com/sites/victorlipman/2014/02/21/6-reasons-effective-management-requires-balance/.

Logan, Firourzeh F. 2009. "A Brief History of Reference Assessment: No Easy Solutions." *The Reference Librarian* 50, no. 3: 225–33.

Matthews, Joseph R. 2007. *Library Assessment in Higher Education*. Westport, CT: Libraries Unlimited.

Nicholas, David, Ian Rowlands, Michael Jubb, and Hamid R. Jamali. 2010. "The Impact of the Economic Downturn on Libraries: With Special Reference to University Libraries." *Journal of Academic Librarianship* 36, no. 5: 376–82.

Novotny, Eric. 2010. "Hard Choices in Hard Times: Lessons from the Great Depression." *Reference & User Services Quarterly* 49, no. 3: 222–24.

Saunders, Laura. 2013. "Learning from Our Mistakes: Reflections on Customer Service and How to Improve It at the Reference Desk." *College & Undergraduate Libraries* 20, no. 2, 144–55.

CHAPTER 6

Marketing and Collaboration for Reference Services

Reaching Out from Reference Services

IT IS UNFORTUNATE THAT SOME OBSERVERS have come to view libraries as warehouses of antiquities—dim places filled with moldy books and yellowing newspapers, of interest primarily to white-haired scholars trapped in the past. The richer truth is that libraries are living entities, continuously evolving in response to their environments. They are called upon to preserve the past, embody the present, and envision the future—and most accomplish their mission admirably, despite thin budgets and inconsistent support. To adapt so successfully, it is crucial that libraries embrace every opportunity to interact effectively with the communities and institutions they serve. No library can survive in isolation; therefore every library must find ways to form positive relationships with a wide range of stakeholders and potential partners.

It is natural that reference services should play a major role in library outreach. Reference services are, after all, a primary point of contact for the library. Patrons often turn to the library to obtain advice and resources for their research, and their first stop is usually the reference desk or other reference service point. For this reason, reference services represent a natural bridge between the library and its community; the positive impressions and relationships built through reference transactions can, when nurtured properly, grow into highly productive partnerships.

The process of developing such partnerships sometimes occurs through sheer coincidence and luck—a matter of the right people meeting at the right time and saying the right things. More frequently, however (and more reliably), strategic partnerships and relationships are formed through a deliberate, orderly process of outreach. A well-planned outreach program can provide a variety of benefits: it helps raise the visibility of the library, increases approval from both the community and library administrators, and assists in building support for library funding and other needs. On the whole, outreach is an effective means of keeping libraries connected to their communities and institutions.

The first step in creating any type of outreach program is deciding what you want your program to do. The objectives do not need to be specific in the beginning, but you should be able to articulate your goals in broad terms. You may, for example, wish to form new relationships across the campus or community, or you may want to increase usage for specific resources. You may have multiple goals for your program, but keep in mind that each additional objective will require an equivalent investment of time and other resources. This process of creating a rough set of preliminary goals will help to guide the development of your outreach program.

Before proceeding, however, be aware that some libraries may already have a person or a group responsible for outreach. Complicating this situation are the many titles this responsibility might carry, such as outreach coordinator, communications director, marketing group, and others. It is also possible that someone with an entirely unrelated job title was assigned this responsibility. Find out if someone else is doing outreach in your library before acting on your own—obviously, you don't want to begin a relationship-building program by damaging relationships within your own organization. If someone is handling outreach in your library, ask for a meeting to discuss existing activities or programs. In some instances they will welcome your help and input; in others, they may not regard reference services as relevant to their efforts. Some outreach programs are, for example, tightly focused on obtaining funds through major contributors and grants, and they may not perceive a role for reference services in their plans.

Once you have checked with interested parties in your own organization and made sure you are not infringing on the job duties of others, you are ready to create an outreach program centered on reference services. It is advisable to begin by assigning responsibility for outreach to a specific person. Perhaps you are the best person to lead the project, or you may identify someone else who is better situated to invest the time and effort. The person you choose needs to possess the aptitudes and interests appropriate to the task. Depending on the goals set for your program, this may be someone outgoing and socially adept, with strong interpersonal skills, or it may be a person with the organizational skills to develop and maintain an effective program. Ideally, it would be someone possessing at least some measure of both skill sets. Above all, it should be someone able to work in close collegial relationships with others, both within and outside of the library.

When you have developed a rough idea of your outreach goals and you have a project leader in place, it is time to proceed with development of an outreach program. There are many ways to approach library outreach; two of the most useful for reference services— marketing and collaboration—are described in some detail below.

Marketing is a relatively loose term that has been defined in hundreds of ways. Marketing consultant Heidi Cohen (2011) has, in fact, gathered over 70 definitions of marketing on her website. Among the best is a definition from Renee Blodgett, CEO and founder of Magic Sauce Media: "Marketing is an ongoing communications exchange with customers in a way that educates, informs and builds a relationship over time." This definition, while brief and very simple, includes many of the most important elements of marketing for reference services:

- The primary activity of reference services marketing is communication with your patrons.
- Communication must be ongoing, not a one-time activity.
- Communication should be interactive, with the audience taking an active role in providing feedback and direction.
- Communication should be purposeful and productive—it should educate and inform in a useful way.
- The ultimate objective of marketing is a relationship with your clients and community, built and maintained over time.

The above definition provides a good summary of marketing as it relates to reference services, though it does require some adjustment. While communication is probably the central issue in marketing for reference services, it is also necessary to consider the more traditional purpose of marketing—to assemble the best goods and services possible, in order to present them in the most positive light to the most appropriate group of customers. While many librarians and library administrators reject the use of commercial terms like "customers" for library users, there is no escaping the fundamental purpose of library marketing—increasing awareness and consumption of library resources and services, or, to use the more blunt term, selling. Money does not change hands directly in most library transactions, but the value of the services and products you provide for your patrons will almost certainly have an impact on the efforts of the library to justify its funding, or even its continued existence. Though it may be a bitter pill for some librarians to swallow, selling is indeed a critical aspect of librarianship in the current environment.

Creating a Marketing Plan

Once you have decided to carry out marketing activities to enhance the visibility and usage of your services, the best way to ensure consistent success is to form a carefully considered marketing plan. The purpose of the marketing plan is to guide marketing efforts to achieve your objectives in the most efficient, methodical manner possible. The entire marketing cycle is shown in figure 6.1. Each of the separate steps will be explained in the sections that follow, but the main point to take from this illustration is that each step of the marketing process feeds into the next, and in turn the entire cycle feeds into those that follow; information from a previous cycle is used to improve the effectiveness of the next.

A marketing plan does not need to be either complicated or heavily funded to work well. The marketing relationship, like any relationship, requires listening attentively to others, working to provide good value, and building trust over time through honest,

Figure 6.1.   The marketing cycle

ethical practice. Below are several important things to keep in mind as you develop a marketing plan for reference services.

Market Identification

The first step in developing a marketing plan is identifying who, what, and where your market really is. This will vary for each type of library (academic, public, school, or special), and it will also vary by individual library. Every library has its own unique clientele and environment. Most public university libraries are, for example, required to provide some level of access for non-affiliated users, because they are supported by taxpayers. Private universities, on the other hand, may limit public access to the library, allowing only university-affiliated users and perhaps visiting scholars to use the library's resources. Below are some general examples of the markets served in various types of libraries, but these are only a few suggestions designed to help you start thinking about the specific people your library serves. For any individual library, you must carefully consider who actually uses the library, who might use the library if access were improved, and what other parties have a stake in the library's presence in the community or organization.

- *Academic and research libraries.* University and college libraries do, of course, serve their own affiliated students and faculty, but they might also provide services for staff members, community users, visiting scholars, alumni, donors, local businesses, and community organizations. In addition, they often have cooperative or consortial relationships with other educational institutions, and many academic libraries sell various types of "friends of the library" memberships that include access to library services and resources.
- *Public libraries.* In broad terms, the mission of most public libraries is to serve anyone who walks through the door, but there are some obvious priorities. Public libraries normally focus on their specific geographic parameters, be it state, county, city, or neighborhood. They may also offer extended services and mobile libraries for isolated populations who cannot otherwise use the library. In some cases, public libraries offer augmented services and resources for specific groups, such as literacy initiatives, readers' clubs, or those carrying out specialized research in topics like genealogy or local history.
- *School libraries.* Libraries serving K–12 are focused on the needs of their students, offering research assistance, supporting classroom curriculum, and providing users with a positive initial experience using the library. They serve students, teachers, teaching assistants, school administrators, and occasionally parents or other family members.
- *Corporate or company libraries.* More than almost any other type of library, corporate libraries have a tightly defined clientele, usually consisting exclusively of company employees. Occasionally a corporate library may work in cooperation with other private or government organizations, but its primary mission is almost always supplying information, data, and research services for employees of the company.
- *Other special libraries.* A number of libraries serve specific needs and interests, including medical libraries, theological libraries, law libraries, and others. Identifying a market for these special libraries seems easy given the distinctive nature of their collections, but sometimes it is not. Some of the more famous special libraries—the Folger Shakespeare Library in Washington, DC, the Vatican Library in Rome— attract scholars and researchers from all over the world. As with any other kind of library, special libraries must carefully consider not only their primary audience, but also the untapped potential markets waiting to be discovered.

Market Segments

"One size fits all" is generally a poor approach to marketing. At the beginning of this section, marketing was identified as a form of communication leading ultimately to a positive relationship. Great relationships with your patrons are rarely built on cookie-cutter communication that does not connect with the audience in a personal way. Once you have identified the market you serve, or wish to serve, it is important to determine how many different subgroups or segments should be separated from the overall market. There are many ways to segment a market, but when marketing for library reference services, the focus should be on speaking directly to the needs and interests of specific groups of library users. In a public library, for example, the marketing activities you would undertake to increase attendance at a weekly story hour for preschool children would be different from those you might use to increase awareness of a collection of rare historical documents. There is, of course, a limit on the number of marketing segments you would want to reach separately. Returning to the example of a public library, it might be helpful to separate children's marketing from marketing aimed at business researchers, but it would probably not be necessary to separate the business researchers by personal income or specific industries. The business researchers will have similar interests, and in all but the largest public libraries they will use similar library resources to carry out research.

The number of marketing segments you wish to recognize should be based on practical considerations. In an academic library, for example, faculty members generally undertake deeper, more comprehensive research than do their students. Obviously, the reference services provided to each group should reflect these differences. It is also important to determine the best methods to communicate with each group. Would you reach students using the same media you would use to reach faculty? A recent study of millennials (the generation born after the advent of the digital era) found that 85 percent of respondents believe it is important to keep up with the news, but 86 percent also indicated that that they get most of their news from social media—such as friends' posts on Facebook, Twitter, and similar sites (Media Insight Project, 2015). Marketing to college students would, therefore, require focusing on their specific reference needs, as well as communicating with them through appropriate channels.

Figure 6.2 provides a visual representation of breaking your market into segments. This diagram indicates that each segment may require its own marketing research process, its own marketing activity plan, and its own process of evaluation and revision. As you decide on the number of marketing segments, you should keep in mind that each segment will require time-consuming individual work and attention to be effective. The number of marketing segments may, in other words, be limited as much by the resources you have at your disposal as by the perceived need for separate marketing plans. Take into account the benefits and costs of adding segments before committing scarce resources that may provide limited returns on the required investment.

Market Research

Having given some thought to the makeup of your market, and the segments into which it should be divided, your next task is to learn as much as you can about the people your library serves. For each market segment, you will need to develop a clear profile of what your clientele wants, and how best to deliver it. The process of researching your market will, therefore, require appropriate planning and prioritization. What follows are several of the more important points to consider as you form your research plan.

- *Managerial vs. scholarly research.* As you review the scholarly literature on market research, it is important to remember that you are performing research to achieve practical objectives. You wish to know more about your library clients and patrons, and to use this knowledge to improve the delivery of services and resources. Most scholarly research, on the other hand, is designed to carry out theoretical inquiries that may not be relevant to the everyday concerns of library reference services. Keep your research focused on the needs of reference services.

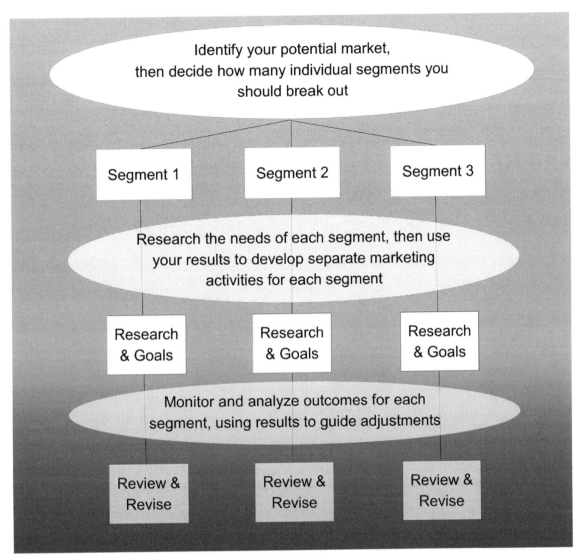

Figure 6.2. Breaking the market into separate segments

- *Informal vs. formal.* Marketing research is a broad term covering many types of activities. Market research can be an involved, time-consuming, expensive process, or it can be a relatively informal affair requiring only a few hours. You should undertake an honest self-appraisal of your needs before you begin any marketing research project. You don't want to waste resources on an overblown research project, nor do you want to rush through a slapdash effort that does not yield useful results.
- *Existing data vs. new data.* The scope of the research required for your marketing efforts will be largely determined by deciding whether you need to carry out original research to gather data, or can use existing data. In many cases, your library or the reference staff will possess data on reference services. Many libraries complete extensive surveys of their users on a regular basis, and many of the items they survey may apply directly to marketing reference services. You may, for example, find data on user ratings of reference services and resources going back many years, and this can save you considerable effort (for a detailed discussion of data collection practices and procedures, see the section titled "Assessing Reference Services" in chapter 5).
- *Know the library and its users.* Whatever method you choose for gathering information, review your data carefully to gain a full picture of reference services and

reference users. Examine past and present ratings of reference services and consider all sources—the good, the bad, and even the ugly—to inform decisions about future marketing activities. Look for insights on what your users want, but give even greater consideration to the things they really need. Look for obstacles that are stopping your clients from using your library and its resources, and remove those obstacles where feasible.

- *When enough is enough.* As important as it is to collect information about your users, it is equally important to know when you have enough. You will never know everything about your users, and there is a point where too much data and analysis can result in overthinking your topic. It may be helpful to stop occasionally and perform a mental calculation of the potential costs and benefits of carrying out further research. When you find yourself facing diminishing returns on useful data as research costs increase, it is time to stop. In the end, you must trust your intuition and move forward, knowing that you can make adjustments if and when it becomes necessary.

Defining Services and Products

Market research will tell you a great deal about a library's users, but it will also help gauge the effectiveness of services and resources currently offered by the library. Remember that marketing is not limited to selling or advertising—it also involves supplying the best selection of products and services to your customer. User-preference data can be used to guide changes and adjustments to the library's offerings, bringing them into better alignment with user priorities. In some cases, this might result in major restructuring of services, though more often the appropriate response would consist of small refinements, like adjusting hours of operation or updating specific library resources. It is crucial, however, to let the data drive decisions, and to avoid overreacting to random complaints that may not represent a significant proportion of your users.

It is also important to make a distinction between user wants and needs. Which changes could make the difference between your library patrons coming to the library or staying home? A library user may request additional titles by an author who has caught his or her attention, though the user will probably continue visiting the library if this request is not granted. A patron who needs to use computers in the library might, on the other hand, stop coming if there are too few computers available, or if there is a long wait to use them. When in doubt, best practice is to include items in your user surveys that touch on these issues. You might use some form of rating scale for this purpose. Figure 6.3 is an example of a more traditional rating scale. In this case, the respondent indicates how important she

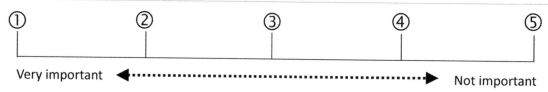

Figure 6.3. Example of a traditional rating scale

REMEMBERING THE SCIENTIFIC METHOD

When performing research for practical applications like reference services, it is easy to forget the basis of all inquiry—the scientific method. Many marketing topics can be researched effectively using informal methods, but occasionally a question arises that requires a more rigorous treatment. As a reminder, the steps involved in scientific research are shown below.

1. *State a research question.* State the problem you wish to resolve. This may involve questions such as "what factors control whether a researcher will come to the library to find resources?"
2. *Gather existing information and data.* Try to find answers for your question. There may be existing research or data on the subject, or you may wish to ask colleagues and other experts for advice. In the example above, you might find research articles in journals related to librarianship, or you may find practical answers by speaking to staff within your own library.
3. *Create a hypothesis.* Use the information and data obtained to form an educated guess to answer your research question. In this case, for example, you might hypothesize that previous education about library resources and skills may affect patrons' decisions about coming to library to perform research.
4. *Test your hypothesis.* Decide on a method to prove or disprove (or at least find support for) the guesses you have made to explain your research questions. For example, find a class that is doing a library research project, and ask how many of the students have received library instruction or training. Then ask the same group how many of them went to the library to get help with projects. You could repeat this exercise in several classes to see if the results are consistent and reproducible.
5. *Analyze your results.* When you have gathered your data, find out if they support your hypothesis. In high-level research applications, this analysis might require advanced statistical techniques, but for most issues in reference services a simple examination of the data will tell you what you need to know.
6. *Report your results.* When you have completed your testing and analysis, report your results. In some cases, this may rise to the level of publishing your results in a professional or academic journal, but at the least you should write up a report on your research so people within your organization can refer to your results when needed, or so they can replicate your methodology in the future.
7. *Repeat the process as needed.* Ideally, the results of your study will be used to guide improvements to your services or make changes to your marketing activities. Once these changes have been implemented, you may wish to repeat the inquiry process to determine how effective the changes have been, and to help make continued improvements. You can repeat this cycle as often as the situation demands.

perceives a library instant chat service, using a five-point scale where 1 is "not important at all," and 5 is "very important." This type of scale is easy to create and easy to print or produce in digital format.

In many situations, it may be desirable to present the rating scale in a more illustrative manner, as shown in figure 6.4. Like the more traditional form, this rating scale also allows the respondent to express the perceived importance of library chat service, but the bars provide a graphic representation of increasing importance, and the suggested responses allow the patron to choose specific feelings about instant chat, rather than choosing numbers.

This second approach may appeal to respondents who are not as comfortable with numerical data. In other cases, the suggested responses could be offered in the form of facial expressions (smiles versus frowns) or other pictorial representations. The form of this or any other survey instrument should be designed to make responding easy and pleasurable for your patrons.

Defining Marketing Goals

When you have identified the market and market segments you wish to reach, and you have done some preliminary research on their needs and preferences, you should be ready to define your marketing goals. This part of the marketing process is essential, yet frequently neglected. In an article that is both amusing and insightful, Ned Potter (2013) makes the comparison between marketing mayonnaise and marketing libraries. Potter relates that he sees advertisements for a popular brand of mayonnaise frequently. If he sees an advertisement for this mayonnaise brand he does not, however, jump up and run to the store to buy it. Only when he needed to buy mayonnaise for a particular recipe and found himself staring at the many mayonnaise choices in the store did he think back to the brand-name mayonnaise in the advertisements. He did not choose the brand name because he was slavishly obedient to advertisements—he bought it because he needed mayonnaise for his own reasons, and he had neither the time nor inclination to test each brand himself. In this case, mayonnaise advertisements provided a useful service by helping resolve the consumer's need for advice.

How important is it to you to be able to communicate with a librarian using an instant chat service? (Circle the answer closest to the way you feel)

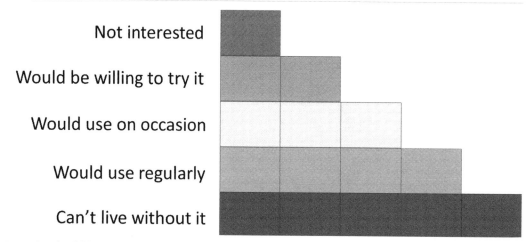

Figure 6.4.   Stacked blocks and verbal descriptions of ratings can make the rating scale more understandable.

Remember this lesson as you plot out marketing goals. First, define the desired outcome of your campaign. Do you want library users to go immediately to the library to ask reference questions, or do you want them to be aware of your services when they do have a need for reference assistance? The latter is a more reasonable goal—you are gradually building awareness of the services available at the library, with the objective of helping patrons recall the options that are open to them when find themselves in need. As a rule, a marketing plan for reference services focuses on one of the following objectives:

- *Increased awareness.* Probably the most common marketing goal is making library users aware of the services and resources available through library reference services. This requires reaching out to users through the most appropriate media. You might reach some of your users with printed flyers or bookmarks, while others will be more likely to read notices through the library website or email, and still others are most accessible through social media.
- *Increased usage.* A more challenging goal is to actually change the behavior of library users. This may amount to creating more hits on a website, initiating more face-to-face interactions at the reference desk, or downloading more electronic journal articles. This will require increasing your users' awareness of services, but you will also need to provide motivation to act. If you are marketing to specific college classes working on a research paper, you could make them aware that reference services can help them find articles and books for their projects. A public library might wish to reach entrepreneurs to tell them that reference services can help with marketing research for their growing businesses. Notice that as your marketing goals become more ambitious, you may have to market to a more specific audience in order to obtain the desired results.
- *Increase support.* Probably the most difficult goal you can set for yourself as a library marketer is changing people's fundamental beliefs about the library. It is one thing to take a library user and increase their knowledge of the library, or even to convince them to use the library in new and unaccustomed ways. It is quite another to take a person who doesn't like libraries (perhaps a bad experience as a child) or who feels money spent on libraries is a poor use of funds, and convert them into a library supporter—or at least less of an opponent. This may require in-depth research to understand the nature of the opposition, and intense campaigning that may include giving talks at events that reach influential members of your community or organization. Working at this level is certainly a challenge, but one that can be rewarding if you are even partially successful.

Decisions on marketing goals may be needed for each separate product or resource you wish to market, and each market segment you wish to reach. Think carefully about what you really wish to accomplish, and be reasonable in your expectations. You will not cause a significant increase in reference transactions by posting a few flyers on campus or sending an email announcement through a mass mailing list. With consistent communication efforts, however, you may build awareness of services that will pay off when someone in your audience faces a real need. This is where marketing research really comes into play—the key is identifying your users' needs and finding solutions for their problems. If you can help solve a real-world problem for your audience, then you have something of value to market.

⊚ Implementing a Marketing Campaign

Having determined your marketing goals, you are now ready to plan your marketing campaign. There are many possible approaches. Much will depend on your knowledge of and intuition for the market—you must have accurate instincts for communicating with your clientele in the right way to achieve the desired results. There are, however, several steps you can follow to get started in the right direction. If you have not previously planned a marketing program, your first efforts may be a little hit or miss, but you can always revise and make adjustments to your campaign, even in mid-process. It is likely that even a clumsy marketing program will increase the visibility of your services. The following sections will offer some basic methods for getting your marketing campaign off and running.

Crafting Your Message

There is a temptation to undervalue the importance of carefully developing your marketing message. Marketing messages are often thrown together quickly and tossed into the world carelessly, because by this point in the marketing process most librarians are convinced that they know what they want to say to their patrons. "Come to the library for your reference needs," the librarian wants to say. "We're better than Google, and just as easy to use!" Sadly, most patrons don't really believe that, and, as it turns out, they don't really care about your efforts to bring more people into the library. The harsh reality is that the only way to reach most of your users is to speak about *their* concerns, not your own.

Creating a truly patron-centered message requires some forethought, and more than a little effort. Below are several important strategies and tips to help you bring your message into focus.

- *Know your audience.* Build your message on a complete knowledge of your users. This is the point where your careful marketing research will pay off. You need to know users well enough to understand the problems they face. It should be relatively easy to do this for library reference services. Review your reference transactions, either by going over records and transcripts, or (more often the case) by simply recalling reference users you and the rest of the reference staff have served. Think about the problems that brought them to the reference desk, particularly those that caused the users considerable distress and anxiety. It is exactly this sort of distress you wish to eliminate for them. You need clear answers to your audience's unspoken question: "What's in it for me?"
- *Know your product.* You must be able to articulate clearly what you can do to solve a pressing problem for your audience, and how reference users can obtain your help quickly and easily. You need to show in a convincing manner that your services are better than those of your competition. Be specific—explain what you can do for them that no one else can, including rare and expensive resources, hard-to-find databases, or a convenient location. An important tip on human behavior: to maximize the impact of your message, clearly identify benefits patrons will be missing by not using the library's services—most people are more motivated to act to avoid loss than to obtain benefits.
- *Make a memorable impression.* The ultimate aim of marketing is to create a lasting positive impression of the library and its services. Carefully consider the underlying image you are trying to convey, using a consistent tone and design in your

marketing materials to maintain it. It is best to keep your message concise, using simple language and active verbs where possible. Pictures and images are, moreover, more memorable than even the catchiest phrases and tag lines. Above all, maintain awareness of the way your audience communicates and use this knowledge to make sure you are reaching them using appropriate language, expressed through appropriate media.

Communicating Your Message

Suppose you are hiring for an important position at your library. An applicant sends you an email stating, "Hey dude, I'm Bob, and I want a job. Just respond to this email with your big-cash offer." Would you hire Bob? Can you think of anyone who would? Bob has, after all, given you absolutely no reason to hire him. You don't know about his work history or education, and he has not told you what he can do for the library or its patrons. The only thing you really know about Bob is that he doesn't understand the most basic rules of professional behavior. Using little more professional savvy than Bob, however, many libraries lay out a few bookmarks printed with the library's phone number and hours of operation, and consider their marketing chores completed. Many years ago, this may have been a workable (if uninspired) strategy, but it is not acceptable in the current environment of budget cuts and library funding battles.

To this point in the chapter, you have learned to identify your market and its segments, and you have considered the message you want to use to highlight appropriate reference services and resources. Now comes the most difficult and important aspect of marketing—taking your message to the market in a way that brings about the desired outcomes. This portion of your marketing plan consists largely of choosing the specific medium (or media) you will employ to communicate your message, along with a general strategy for distributing your marketing resources in a way that maximizes the impact of your message—often referred to as the "marketing mix" (Borden, 1964). When you market library reference services, in principle you are performing the same set of tasks as marketers in for-profit businesses, but in practical terms, libraries use different channels of communication than do their for-profit counterparts. Below are some of the most useful media and methods for library marketing.

- *Personal contact.* One of the most effective means of marketing almost anything is by building personal relationships between those who provide the service and those who use it. For library reference services, every reference transaction is a chance to build a positive experience that can develop into a long-term, mutually beneficial relationship.
- *Instruction.* Most reference librarians provide at least some form of library instruction. This may be limited to one-on-one interactions at a reference desk, or it may include classroom instruction, workshops, and webinars. Effective library instruction sessions can help patrons see the library as a place to learn and develop, not just a place to find books. Many great library relationships are built through these events—patrons often remember librarians from instruction sessions and presentations, and they frequently feel comfortable contacting these librarians later when they have a specific need.
- *Library websites and guides.* In this technologically obsessed era, the library website is an indispensable marketing tool for the library. Nearly every resource used

for library research is accessed through the website, including the catalog. The website must, therefore, be easy to navigate, and the services accessed through it must operate intuitively. Your library should be evaluating the effectiveness of the website frequently to ensure that patrons can find everything they need. Reference services staff should, moreover, possess a thorough knowledge of the contents of the website, and they should be highly skilled at guiding patrons through its many functions and access points.

- *Social media.* These online social applications continue to flourish, and as they do, their use for library outreach is growing as well. Millennials increasingly get their news through social media, but they are not alone. Library users of all ages use social media to communicate and obtain information through an ever-expanding array of specialized apps. For reference services, this is a low-cost, efficient way to reach users who would be difficult to contact through other means. It is necessary, however, to thoroughly research of your target market to confirm that you are using social media appropriately for your users.

- *Other online alternatives.* In addition to websites and social media, there are several other means of connecting with library users. Many libraries maintain library blogs to keep users informed of library news, resources, services, and events. Some of these blogs are run through the library website, while others utilize any of several free systems and are then linked from the library website. A key element of a successful blog is a technologically savvy, enthusiastic staff member who will keep the blog lively, up-to-date, and enjoyable. Other libraries provide an email listserv so users can post questions, which may be answered by other users or by library staff. This often works best when you are serving a population with a shared interest in a specific topic.

- *The brick-and-mortar library.* An encouraging recent trend in libraries is a renewed respect for the library as a physical space. Patrons are rediscovering the joys of working or just relaxing at the library. Use the space in your library to advertise reference services and new resources through bulletin boards and video boards. This is also where you can make use of traditional bookmarks and flyers—distributing information about reference services at points around the building.

- *Promotions and events.* Public, special, and school libraries have long made extensive use of events and promotions, such as book clubs and author appearances, to attract and entertain their patrons. Even academic libraries are using this strategy more extensively, with the goal of providing added value to the campus, and enticing busy students and faculty to visit the library. Any library-sponsored event is an excellent opportunity to remind the audience of library services and resources, and to distribute helpful flyers and brochures.

Assessing Marketing Activities

When you have finished implementing your marketing plan, it is time to review your results. Did everything go as planned, or did you encounter stumbling blocks? Did your plan bring about the desired outcome? What should you do differently next time? Seek thorough, satisfying answers to these questions. This information will help you justify your marketing activities to your superiors, and make the case for additional resources and funding in the future. A thorough review of your activities will also help guide and improve the quality of future marketing plans. It is well worth the effort, therefore, to take the steps below to assess your marketing activities.

1. *Gathering data.* Just as you gathered data to guide decisions in creating your marketing plan, you should now gather data to evaluate its effectiveness. This data must be directly related to your marketing goals. If you set out to increase awareness of library services, for example, you could survey your patrons to find out if they are more aware of services now than before you began your marketing activities. If your goal was to increase the use of reference services, you might compare usage data gathered before and after your marketing plan went into effect. Finding data that accurately reflects the effectiveness of your marketing plan can be difficult in some situations. For instance, you might wish to gather objective data showing that a public library's reference services improve the work performance of its patrons. It would not be reasonable to track the work performance of every person who came to the reference desk. In such cases, practicality may demand that you settle for anecdotal self-reports gathered through patron interviews or surveys. Showing that your patrons *think* their work performance has improved is not as valuable as showing that their performance actually did improve, but it will help to make your case. With a little creativity, you can, in other words, find ways to identify which areas of your marketing program are working effectively, and which need revising.

2. *Analyzing data.* Once you have gathered the best possible data to assess your marketing plan, you need to interpret the meaning of your results. Analysis of data for reference services is usually a fairly straightforward process. You observe an increase in awareness of services among your patrons, or you don't. You see an increase in reference transactions, or you don't. More challenging, however, is determining whether the cost of the marketing plan (in terms of hours, funds, or other resources) is worth the benefits obtained. This is where the objectives you created at the onset of planning your marketing plan will come into play. Suppose you complete six months of labor-intensive marketing activities using the time of multiple staff members, all with the goal of increasing reference traffic. If your efforts result in an additional three reference transactions over the six-month period, you would be unlikely to call it a resounding victory. Now is the time to look again at your project goals, remaining faithful to the standards of success you created at the onset. Do not surrender to the temptation to change your goals in a vain attempt to sugar-coat results. Allowing the results to speak for themselves will provide your library with valid feedback to guide the creation of future marketing plans, and will yield greater benefits over time.

3. *Revise and repeat.* Using your analysis of previous marketing efforts, along with renewed consideration of the current needs of the library, you can now adjust future marketing efforts to more effectively cultivate and improve your library's services. Ideally, this process should repeat continuously, keeping the marketing cycle closely aligned with the changing needs, challenges, and opportunities faced by your library.

Collaboration

Another way library reference services are extending their reach and stretching resources involves entering collaborative arrangements, both within the library system and with external parties. For the purposes of the current discussion, a workable definition of collaboration comes from BusinessDictionary.com (2016), which describes it as "a cooperative arrangement in which two or more parties work jointly towards a common goal." While brief, this definition covers the essential elements of collaboration. First, the collaboration must be cooperative, with all parties shouldering an equivalent share of the planning, funding, labor, and oversight. Second, all parties should agree to work together as a group, rather than pursuing differing and sometimes conflicting approaches. Finally, and most important, all parties must agree on a shared objective, with at least some fundamental consensus on the definition and parameters of that objective.

Many libraries view collaboration as an appropriate response to painful cuts in resources and staffing. By breaking down traditional walls between the library and groups or agencies with compatible goals, library leaders see the potential to reap many benefits. Effective collaboration can spread talent and resources more efficiently, and it can avoid duplication of function. By pooling people and resources, libraries can increase their visibility on campuses and in communities, and they can increase the quality and availability of the services they offer.

On the other side of the equation, libraries bring valuable assets to their partners. Libraries are almost universally regarded as indispensable pillars of a modern, democratic society—a non-partisan, reliable source of objective information and data, available without charge or restrictions. Librarians are trained and experienced in finding and retrieving information on almost any subject, from practical topics like business and health to the most arcane areas of the arts and sciences. Libraries also provide free access to physical spaces, including meeting rooms, work areas, and computer labs.

Is Collaboration the Right Solution?

When arranged thoughtfully and managed effectively, collaborations can produce many benefits, but they can be counterproductive when thrown together carelessly and allowed to drift from their initial intent. Before rushing into a collaborative partnership, management scholar Morten T. Hansen (2009) suggests carefully analyzing the likelihood of receiving what he calls a "collaboration premium." For a library, this would involve considering the benefits you expect to receive from the collaboration, then subtracting the resources you would expend (e.g., time, effort, and funds) carrying out the collaboration. This result—the net benefit of the project—must then be compared to all the alternative projects in which you might invest your resources. Only if the collaboration promises more net benefits than any other option—a collaboration premium—would you agree to take part. Even if you do not wish to pursue an evaluation process like that proposed by Hansen, you should still take a moment to make a mental calculation of the real benefits and costs of any potential partnership. A successful collaboration demands considerable time, patience, and diplomacy. A failed collaboration includes the risk of alienating groups or organizations with which your library has maintained positive relations for many years. Consider all of the variables carefully before deciding if collaboration is the best way to reach your goals.

In addition to the tangible costs of collaboration described above, it would be wise to consider the cumulative effects of collaborative projects on the most committed members of the reference staff. Research indicates that up to 35 percent of the value created by collaborations results from the efforts of 3 percent to 5 percent of the staff (Cross, Rebele, and Grant, 2016). These researchers also note that, overall, the use of collaborative projects has increased by over 50 percent in the last two decades. This means that the increasing demand for collaborative projects is being borne on the backs of a very small percentage of the staff—usually the best and most productive members. To avoid the risks of burnout and turnover among your best staff members, it is necessary to take careful stock of the number of collaborations underway at a given time.

None of the above should be taken, however, as a condemnation of collaborative partnerships for reference services. While it is certainly wise to scrutinize the pros and cons of collaborative opportunities carefully, many collaborations create considerable value for libraries and are well worth all the costs involved.

Developing Effective Collaborations

The key to making collaborations work effectively is identifying the kinds of partnerships appropriate to your needs and environment. For example, Erin E. Meyer (2014) of the University of Denver notes that her library obtained the best results by focusing on short-term, project-based collaborations with campus partners—the "low-hanging fruit," as she describes it. This may hold particularly true for library reference services. The need for involved collaborative programs is often carried out at higher levels of library administration than reference services (such as consortium purchases of major electronic resources, or selecting library management systems). Reference services may benefit from more humble arrangements, such as author lectures, movie screenings, or instructional sessions on library-related topics outside of the library facilities. These types of collaborations may afford worthwhile benefits while demanding few resources. Such casual partnerships are also a good way to try working with new partners—successful outcomes for small projects may indicate the potential for bigger projects in the future.

Flexibility is another useful strategy for finding the best collaborations. Remain open to the emergence of collaborative partnerships outside normal channels. These serendipitous opportunities can provide unexpected potential for mutual benefit. In helping a patron find information on an obscure subject, for instance, you might locate a local expert who would be delighted to provide a presentation or instruction session on a specialized topic. This arrangement could be the beginning of a highly rewarding partnership that helps the library offer an expanded service, provides patrons with a valuable source of information, and allows the expert to find new clients and followers—all thanks to an awareness of the possibilities that can open up every day. Below are several more general strategies that may help when developing effective collaborations.

- *Get permission.* When forming collaborations, it is important to let library administrators know what you are doing. By entering agreements with other parties, you are bringing the library into those agreements with you. Make sure you have support for the arrangements you are planning, and for the partners you are bringing into those arrangements. Even if your library tends to be supportive of collaborations, your library administrators deserve to be made aware of your activities, as they may be called on to answer for them if something goes awry.
- *Know your library.* Understand the nature and identity of your library, and keep this in mind as you consider collaborations. Maintain awareness of your library's mission and its fundamental values, and be sure they are compatible with activities you will undertake and organizations with which you will partner.
- *Take organizational cultures into account.* Different libraries and organizations develop different ways of doing things. While your collaborators may be good at what they do, and ethical in the way they do it, it is still important to confirm

that the cultures can coexist. An academic library could, for example, have a relaxed, supportive culture at odds with an aggressive, competitive company culture in the private sector. All collaborations are, at the end of the day, personal relationships—make sure the various parties in a collaboration are able to work together in a positive, professional environment.

- *Know what you want to get done.* Returning to the theme of cost/benefit discussed earlier in this section, as you begin a collaboration it is important to maintain a keen awareness of the needs of your library and those of your partners. Your objectives do not have to be identical, but they must be compatible to the point that a collaborative project will produce a net benefit for all parties.

- *Consider a written agreement.* If you are entering a complex collaborative arrangement, or if you see the potential for misunderstandings in what is otherwise a beneficial project, consider creating written documentation of the agreement. Outline the objectives of the collaboration, along with the responsibilities and expectations for all participants. Define the limits of the project—a clear statement of what constitutes success or failure, and restrictions on total investment in terms of time and other resources. Be particularly careful in spelling out financial aspects of the agreement. Make sure everyone understands clearly how much funding will be expected from each participant and, if proceeds are expected, how they will be handled and distributed. By setting explicit boundaries at the beginning of a collaboration, you can reduce the likelihood of unpleasant exchanges as the project heats up. Remember, however, to maintain enough flexibility to permit fluid adjustment to unexpected circumstances. A very basic example of a memorandum of understanding, involving a hypothetical collaboration at an imaginary university, is shown in the box below. Note that even in this brief example the parties are clearly identified, the purpose and benefits of the collaboration are spelled out, and the responsibilities of all parties are made explicit.

- *Set reasonable timelines.* Move quickly and efficiently toward your goals, but don't allow the project to fall into an unnecessarily stressful cycle of unrealistic deadlines and excessive expectations. Leave time to deal with contingencies in a reasonable manner. You should, in fact, incorporate extra time into the plan to accommodate the inevitable delays that result from negotiating and planning among collaborative partners.

Types of Collaborations

When entering a collaborative arrangement, consider the various types of collaborations that might be applicable in your situation. A formal collaboration between library reference services and a campus writing center, incorporating agreements on the specific obligations of all parties, dates of operation, and staffing levels during peak hours, might look different from an informal partnership with a local book club arranging to meet in a room at the local library. Many knowledgeable authors have created lists of types of collaboration, each with its own unique perspective. For the purpose of library-related collaborations, most of the following have been adapted from the work of blogger Deb Lavoy (2010):

- *Creative collaborations.* Here, the primary objective is to create or develop something. This might involve a collaboration with information technology staff to

[SAMPLE] MEMORANDUM OF UNDERSTANDING

Parties to the Collaboration
1) *Veritas University Library Reference Services*, 100 Campus Way, College Town, NY

   The University Library Reference Services (hereafter referenced as the Library) provides research assistance and reference services to VU faculty, students, staff, and community users.
2) *Veritas University Writing Center*, 200 College Blvd., College Town, NY

   The University Writing Center (hereafter referenced as the Writing Center) sponsored by the English Department, assists students as they plan, organize, and revise class papers and projects.

Purpose and Benefits
The Library and the Writing Center have agreed to form a collaborative arrangement whereby the Writing Center will be given space in the Library to assist students with class papers and projects. This collaboration will expand services to students as they work on their papers in the library, meeting their needs at the time and place most convenient for them. It will allow both the Library and the Writing Center to carry out their respective missions more effectively.

Timeframe
This collaboration will be carried out on a trial basis for the 2017–2018 academic year. In July 2018 all parties will review the results and decide whether to continue in the future.

Responsibilities and Roles
The Library agrees to:
1) Provide Writing Center staff with appropriate desk space, two office chairs, a computer and printer in good working condition, and such reference works as are appropriate.
2) Provide security and IT support as needed and appropriate.
3) Notify the Writing Center of any changes in hours for holidays, special events, weather closings, and other contingencies.

The Coordinator of the Library Information Commons will be responsible for upholding the Library's portion of this agreement and will meet with the Writing Center director at least once per semester to discuss the progress and status of the collaboration.

The Writing Center agrees to:
1) Provide 20 hours of staffing at the Library per week, on days and hours agreeable to both parties.
2) Maintain records of the number of students served, to be shared with the Library.
3) Notify the Library of occasions when Writing Center staff cannot fulfill agreed-upon hours at the Library.

The Director of the Writing Center will be responsible for upholding the Writing Center's portion of this agreement and will meet with the Library Information Commons Coordinator at least once per semester to discuss the progress and status of the collaboration.

Signature (Library Information Commons Coordinator):

_____Date_____

Signature (Writing Center Director):

_____Date_____

create video presentations and tutorials for the library, or a collaboration with local artists to produce posters or artwork for the library. The collaboration will have a specific product or goal as its end result, often using the collective talents and time of the participants to accomplish something beyond the abilities of the individual partners.

- *Connective collaborations.* This type describes a more open collaborative arrangement in which the members may not work together directly, or even know each other. This could be a group of subject experts assembled by the library to assist those seeking advanced knowledge on a specific topic. Some libraries have a group of experts who volunteer to share knowledge with people starting a new business, or creating a new public service group. The experts provide knowledge to help get new and beneficial projects off the ground. For other topics or issues, online forums may provide similar access to specialized knowledge that might be available through other sources.

- *Compounding collaboration.* This is a type of collaboration in which participants use existing knowledge as a foundation on which to build to new heights. One example might be succession planning within the organization—the use of mentoring or apprenticeships to pass along knowledge that will keep the organization growing into the future. An obvious example is leading your patrons to articles and studies written about a topic of interest. This allows patrons to use the knowledge gathered by previous researchers to make further strides in their field of study. In most cases the library patrons do not know the authors personally—the authors may, in some cases, have died centuries before—but this doesn't stop them from collaborating effectively, even if it is across time.

- *Library consortia.* To Lavoy's three main types of collaboration must be added a form of collaboration familiar to almost all librarians. A consortium of libraries is a collaborative arrangement most often centered around obtaining discounted pricing on major library resources including databases, library management systems, and other resources. Consortia also provide members with opportunities to network and create additional collaborations and partnerships, as well as providing training and professional development.

⊙ Key Points

Libraries are increasingly asked to prove their worth to the communities, campuses, schools, and organizations that support them. This chapter offers a range of suggestions to assist library reference services increase their value, both within the library system and to the patrons they serve.

- Increasing the visibility and stature of library reference services requires conscious planning and effort, with a clear picture of your goals and limitations.
- To increase awareness of the library and its resources, the most effective course is to create a thorough marketing plan based on strategic planning, efficient marketing research, and a detailed proposal for reaching your marketing goals.
- Marketing efforts must be an ongoing process in which a consistent message is gradually honed through repeated cycles of delivery, assessment, and revision.

- Another important method of increasing the reach of library reference services is through the creation of effective, well-planned collaborations with appropriate partners.

The next chapter will look forward, examining the future of reference services.

⑥ References

Borden, Neil H. 1964. "The Concept of the Marketing Mix." *Journal of Advertising Research* 4, no. 2: 7–12.

BusinessDictionary.com. 2016. "Collaboration." http://www.businessdictionary.com/definition/collaboration.html.

Cohen, Heidi. 2011. "72 Marketing Definitions." *Actionable Marketing Guide* (blog), March 29. http://heidicohen.com/marketing-definition/.

Cross, Rob, Reb Rebele, and Adam Grant. 2016. "Collaborative Overload." *Harvard Business Review* 94, no. 1: 74–79.

Hansen, Morten T. 2009. "When Internal Collaboration Is Bad for Your Company." *Harvard Business Review* 87, no. 4: 82–88.

Lavoy, Deb. 2010. "It's Not the Same Thing: The 3 Types of Collaboration." *ProductFour* (blog), March 20. https://productfour.wordpress.com.

Media Insight Project. 2015. "How Millennials Get Their News: Inside the Habits of America's First Digital Generation." *American Press Institute*, March 16. https://www.americanpressinstitute.org/publications/reports/survey-research/millennials-news/.

Meyer, Erin E. 2014. "Low-Hanging Fruit: Leveraging Short-Term Partnerships to Advance Academic Library Outreach Goals." *Collaborative Librarianship* 6, no. 3: 112–20.

Potter, Ned. 2013. "Marketing Libraries Is Like Marketing Mayonnaise." *Library Journal*, April 18. http://lj.libraryjournal.com/2013/04/opinion/advocates-corner/marketing-libraries-is-like-marketing-mayonnaise/#_.

The Future of Reference Services

Is Reference Dead?

IN THE CURRENT ENVIRONMENT, ANY DELIBERATION of the future of reference services must begin by considering whether there will actually *be* a future for reference services. After all, numerous critics have pointed out that most of the questions commonly asked of reference librarians can now be answered with a quick search on Google or Wikipedia. If you need to know the population of France, for example, Google can answer immediately. If you would like to read a brief biography of Alexander Hamilton, Wikipedia can supply one in seconds. As early as 1995, Ewing and Hauptman pondered whether traditional reference services were obsolete. They noted that a human reference librarian is susceptible to making mistakes, and can only serve one person at a time. These authors looked toward a brave new future where library users could enjoy interacting with a "holographic librarian operating in a virtual universe" (6). Lewis (1995) castigated much of Ewing and Hauptman's reasoning, yet arrived at a similar vision of the electronic library of the future, when human-to-human reference interactions have been largely eliminated.

In the 20 years that have passed since these articles were written, librarians continue to be human, not holographic, and they continue to serve living, breathing patrons at the library. There is no question, however, that the reference services environment has changed in fundamental ways. Most libraries report the number of reference transactions trending downward in recent years. In some libraries, reference staff spend the majority of their time explaining where the restrooms are, fixing staplers, and clearing paper jams in the copiers and printers. A few libraries have gone so far as to eliminate the reference desk altogether, opting for alternative approaches such as roving reference assistance or reference consultation by appointment.

Based on these observations, some library leaders have even suggested that libraries abandon their traditional role as providers of books and information. Michael Gorman declares that libraries "are not and never have been primarily about information" (2012: 122). He writes that libraries are nothing less than the hearts of their communities, and as such are the gatekeepers of knowledge, with responsibility for such broad functions as literacy and instruction. Gorman proposes that the best way forward for libraries is collaboration with institutions possessing a similar mission and ethos, such as museums, art galleries, and archives. Influential library designer and architect David Adjaye takes a similarly interactive approach, noting that "libraries have changed from a place to deposit public knowledge, to places that house the process of socializing to gain knowledge" (Koerber, 2016). He designs libraries to be part of a "network of support systems," with the goal of increasing community pride and engagement.

Alternatively, library visionary R. David Lankes suggests that modern libraries are losing their place in society because they have become "institutions of remediation" (2012: 12). According to this theory, libraries have adjusted their mission to focus on resolving certain shortcomings in our society. Traditionally, libraries provided extensive collections of books and other materials to those who could not afford to buy them. People now find information online, and they entertain themselves through a variety of broadcast and Internet media. Their need for libraries is reduced. In response, libraries have attempted to revive their usefulness by providing support to campuses and communities in the form of computer and Internet access, workspaces, meeting rooms, tutoring in a variety of skills, and many other services. Lankes cautions, however, that taxpayers and funding groups may eventually decide that there are agencies better equipped than libraries to fill these social needs. Rather than attempting to provide Band-Aids for broad societal shortcomings, he suggests that libraries use their own best talents and resources to help patrons succeed. The focus must remain, in other words, on those things the library does best: supplying patrons with a useful, enjoyable collection of library materials, accompanied by a knowledgeable, well-trained staff to help them make the most of it. While it is possible to quibble with aspects of Lankes's interpretation, there is obvious merit in focusing on what libraries do well, rather than overreaching into areas in which they have no real standing.

There are, in fact, many things libraries continue to do well, and some that they do better than ever. For instance, modern Internet search functions make basic research tasks relatively easy, such as finding out who won last night's baseball game, or how to build a canoe. But in-depth research—the kind required of students performing graduate-level research or entrepreneurs starting a new business—can be far more complicated than at any time in the past. Simply sorting out which research databases to use can be a challenging task in itself, and it is only the first step. Once you have located the right databases or data sets for your needs, you must learn to use them. Some are straightforward, but most electronic library resources are becoming increasingly difficult to master as they provide ever-more comprehensive services. This assumes, moreover, that research databases fulfill the patrons' needs. In many cases, even experienced researchers must consult a dizzying selection of paper and electronic resources, in a wide variety of formats and locations, to answer their queries successfully. As information becomes scattered across so many media, it becomes imperative to find a knowledgeable person to train and guide researchers in proper procedures and strategies. This person could be a paid consultant charging astronomical rates, or a highly trained library professional whose services are paid for collectively by the community or organization, and who provides valuable resources and expertise to anyone with a need. For most researchers, the library professional is the most efficient and economical solution.

The value of librarians working face to face with patrons to supply the answers to research questions remains great, and the skilled reference librarian should remain a vital part of our libraries into the foreseeable future—despite the occasional cynical call for an end to all non-digital library resources and personnel. In order to continue to prosper, however, libraries will need to match their reference services to the real needs of their patrons. As discussed above, future patrons will not need librarians to answer simple questions of fact, or to find out if a particular book is available in the library collection. Kenney suggests that library patrons "want help doing things, rather than finding things" (2015: 21). Patrons will come to the library looking for ways to accomplish their goals. A student will come to the library for help to complete a classroom assignment, while a job-seeker might wish to create an effective résumé. It is critical, therefore, that reference services and reference librarians always appear to be problem solvers and troubleshooters, able to help patrons achieve their objectives and improve their lives. Accepting anything short of this standard will leave libraries open to the level of obsolescence that critics have so gleefully predicted. The sections below offer suggestions and strategies for keeping library reference services active and relevant in an uncertain future.

Facing the Future

Facing Competition

For the past several decades, libraries have been challenged as never before by a powerful assortment of competitors. Library users can find information on the Internet, of course, but they are also using mobile applications and other alternatives to obtain resources formerly available only through libraries. At the same time, libraries must also compete for their share of shrinking budgets across campuses, communities, and organizations, all of which are waging their own battles to maintain adequate funding. The situation is made worse by the tendency of librarians to remain collectively resistant to the concept of competition. Most librarians live to help and support their patrons in any way possible—they have no problem sending them to a source of information outside of the library, if that is the best way to help. Similarly, librarians work hard to use all available funding to provide the best resources possible, but the urge to undercut other departments or agencies to bring home a larger slice of the budget pie is foreign to the thinking of many librarians.

Increasingly, however, librarians are recognizing the necessity to respond effectively to their competitors, in terms of both services and funding. In the future, librarians will need to have a clear understanding of the competitive forces in their environment, along with the knowledge and skills to deal with them. Michael E. Porter (1980) developed what is still generally accepted as the definitive model of competition for an organization or industry. Porter's "five forces" provide insight into the competitive landscape, and they can also form the basis of effective strategies to overcome that competition. Porter created his forces to describe competitive activity in a capitalist free market, so it needs some adjustment to describe the non-profit environment of libraries (note that even corporate libraries operate as support services within their organizations, not as profit centers in any practical sense).

Figure 7.1 illustrates the primary competitive forces, described below, that act on libraries:

- *Internal rivalries.* This term describes competition with other libraries, as well as among departments or groups within your own institution or community. Libraries are not necessarily in competition with other libraries—in fact, many libraries work closely with other libraries to develop mutually beneficial arrangements. Occasionally, though, libraries may end up cannibalizing each other each other to form a consortial arrangement—as when an academic library and public library are eliminated to form a single entity serving both campus and community. This may be proposed as an efficient way to serve the needs of all library users, but it could as easily turn out that all parties are dissatisfied with a library that is neither fish nor fowl, and falls short of the needs of all its users. It is important that every library consistently assess the effectiveness of its services, so it has valid data to present to anyone who questions the library's value or its ability to make a unique contribution. Similarly, it is crucial that libraries engage in consistent, robust marketing programs, so that all stakeholders understand the contributions the library makes to its community.
- *Threat of new competitors.* The key to assessing the threat of new competitors is analyzing the difficulty of "entrance into the market." If you are a public library, for instance, how likely is it that your library system will open a new branch nearby to better serve a growing portion of your community? What if that growing portion of the community includes many of your most active patrons? What if your college campus will face competition from a university opening a branch campus near you?

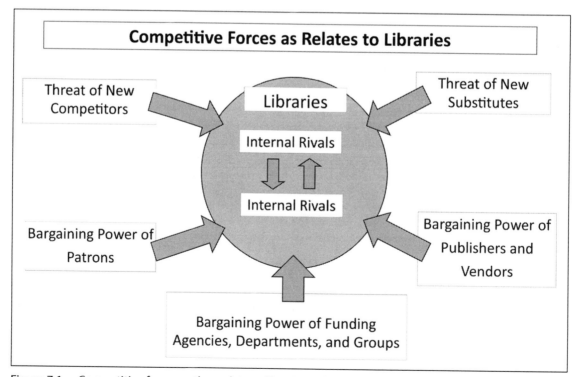

Figure 7.1.   Competitive forces as they relate to libraries. Adapted from Michael Porter's five forces (1980)

In such cases your library could easily see reductions in the number of reference transactions, and this could result in funding and staffing cuts, reductions in hours of operation, or even elimination of services. It is important to have a realistic understanding of the probability that your library will face such challenges, and it is equally important to maintain solid data on the value of your library, as well as good relationships with those in a position to affect your library's future.

- *Threat of new substitutes.* The best-known substitute for library services has been the Internet. The Internet provides an almost unlimited source of information, much of it free to anyone using the computers and open Internet access at their local library, or at any local Wi-Fi hotspot. This is hardly the only possibility for substitutions, however. Amazon and other online services provide free or low-cost access to online books and audiobooks. Various services offer to answer reference questions online, 24 hours a day, 7 days a week, 365 days a year. In the future, any number of mobile apps will offer services—many for free or for a nominal fee—that will overlap with library services. Google's Arts and Culture app, for example, provides instant, searchable access to artworks from over 1,000 museums and galleries. Arts and Culture will eventually connect to Google Cardboard to provide virtual tours of museums, and users will soon be able to enter a photo of a work of art so that the app can search information about it. Libraries must be aware of such changes, certainly, but they must also actively embrace them and help library patrons find and use these new resources.

- *Bargaining power of publishers and vendors.* The ability of any library to serve its patrons depends heavily on effective relationships between the library and the vendors and publishers that sell access to the books, articles, journals, databases, and other resources offered at the library. The companies that provide libraries with both paper and electronic materials have undergone industry disruptions every bit as jarring as those faced by libraries—the business models of textbook publishers are crumbling around them, the publishers of electronic resources seem to undergo almost daily disruptions in their practices, and all parties are stung by shrinking budgets and uncertain futures. Libraries struggle to respond to the astronomical prices of books and electronic databases, and the strength of vendors to place demands on libraries (in terms of both pricing and access policies) will continue to impact the effectiveness of libraries as an institution. Looking to the future, there are several potential strategies under examination. Most libraries are trying to make use of the many free resources available online, linking them to library guides and providing patrons with instruction on using them. Library systems are also using consortial buying arrangements to place pressure on vendors to provide favorable pricing, better products, and more open access to resources. Academic libraries are working to provide open access to faculty journal articles and research through campus repositories, moving slowly toward breaking the stranglehold that major publishers maintain over academic literature. While each of these tactics provides some relief, libraries must remain vigilant in finding new and better methods to maintain their footing against the demands of suppliers.

- *Bargaining power of patrons.* The primary purpose of almost any library is to serve its patrons. From "big picture" strategic documents down to the smallest daily chores, everything done in the library should be tied directly to providing useful services to patrons. Why, then, would the bargaining power of patrons be considered a competitive force? Patron engagement, however desirable it may be in the management of the library, will certainly have an effect on the way the library carries out its work. Patrons may, for example, put pressure on the library to provide reference desk staffing late at night, despite low usage during those hours. This could, in turn, reduce the staffing available during hours of high traffic. As a reference supervisor, the degree to which you may have to acquiesce to the demands of a few patrons at the expense of the majority will impact your ability to maintain high standards for reference services in your library. None of this should be taken to indicate that patron requests are troublesome or counterproductive, but it is important to be able to balance conflicting patron demands to provide the best possible service to the greatest number of patrons. Much of this might best be accomplished by maintaining an open, interactive dialogue with patrons, so that library administrators understand patron needs, and patrons understand the limitations of the library. The creation and inclusion of library patron groups such as advisory councils and steering committees has been very effective for many libraries. It is also helpful to maintain an ongoing program of patron surveys and assessments to provide insight into patron perceptions of the library and its services.

- *Bargaining power of funding agencies.* The critical importance of reliable, responsible funding for libraries cannot be overstated. In recent decades, library funding has become less reliable than in the past. This creates great challenges in providing reliable library services for the public, and in maintaining library collections at their current standards, much less in expanding collections to provide valuable resources, especially online resources. Much of this is due to the forces described above—more competitors and substitutes for library services crop up each day. In the coming years, nearly every library will find itself defending not only its budget requests, but its very existence. For academic and school libraries, this means showing that funds given to the library will help schools achieve goals in retention, graduation, and student achievement. Public libraries will be called on to show how they benefit the constituency they serve, whether municipal, state, or federal, in such areas as general usage, job creation, fostering businesses, serving the underserved, engaging young readers, and improving the standard of life in the community. Corporate and private libraries may face the greatest pressures of all, needing to prove that their funding will have a direct positive effect on their organizations' bottom lines. All libraries need to show that the money spent to keep them operating (and growing) will provide greater benefits than any other potential use of the funds. It is difficult to provide evidence to support such sweeping claims, but libraries must provide the best possible data to show that their programs, services, and collections are providing real benefits. Quantitative evidence, in the form of carefully documented numerical data, is often the most important form of support to present to the people who control funding. It is also helpful, however, to present real-world examples of the library's work through interesting anecdotes, testimonials, and even photos.

There is some controversy over Porter's model, and it should be noted that Porter intended it as an alternative to the SWOT analysis (an analysis of an organization's strengths, weaknesses, opportunities and threats), which he regarded as too loose and informal to use in developing competitive strategies (Argyres and McGahan, 2002). Porter's model is included in this chapter as a general introduction to the concept of strategic competition, but not as a replacement for the SWOT analysis, which is invaluable in assessing library reference services.

Porter later created a model of general strategies that could be used to deal with competitive forces. Figure 7.2 shows Porter's competitive strategy framework, adapted for libraries. Porter believed that there are two basic competitive strategies—competing on cost, and competing to distinguish your products and services from others. He then proposed that both strategies might be carried out either on a broad basis at the industry level, or for a narrow segment of the industry. Further explanation of the terms, adjusted to describe the competitive environment for libraries, is shown below.

- *Differentiation.* This refers to a competitive strategy in which you attempt to separate your library and services from your competitors. In reference services, for example, differentiation could mean offering chat service when your competitors respond only through email. Another approach would be marketing the personal assistance your patrons will receive at the library, as opposed to the faceless, inflexible experience of an online search. Put simply, differentiation means providing your patrons with something better than your competitors can deliver. This could mean better service, a better product, a wider selection of resources, or any other advantage that your patrons would appreciate. Your patrons must be aware of the qualities that differentiate your services from your competitors, and they must value the differences deeply enough to act on them. Consider that some patrons will not value face-to-face service—they might prefer the convenience of finding results online. As with any competitive analysis, you must understand your market completely, and give the market an appropriate mix of services and resources.

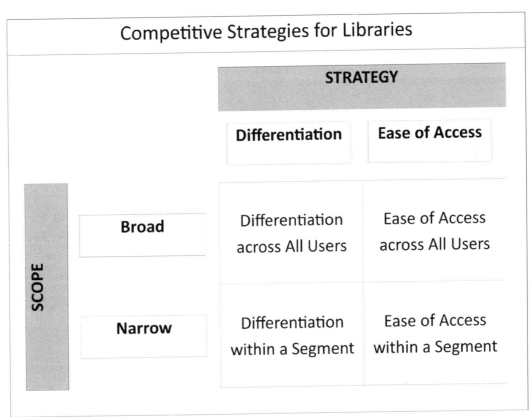

Figure 7.2.   Competitive strategies as they relate to libraries. Adapted from Michael Porter's generic competitive strategies (1980)

- *Ease of access.* This is a form of competitive advantage that replaces "cost leadership" in Porter's original model. Library patrons may not really value cost as a consideration in choosing library resources, as libraries provide most services free or for a nominal charge. This is something many library users fail to appreciate until they try to access journal articles on the Internet, only to encounter demands for an exorbitant fee. Naturally, most library patrons want to obtain their library materials quickly, conveniently, and inexpensively—and most libraries are getting better at responding to these expectations. A patron looking for a book will generally prefer to go to the library for a free copy rather than purchase one from a bookstore. A patron would rather download an article for free from a library database than pay for it online. Remember, however, that most patrons would rather find information quickly through a Google search or Wikipedia article than struggle through a difficult search using library web pages, databases, and catalogs. In the future, libraries must become more adept at providing a fast, intuitive user experience if they are to have any hope of competing with ever-evolving commercial online services.
- *Scope of competition.* A separate dimension of competitive strategic planning is determining the scope of competition you wish to undertake. Porter thought in terms of narrow and broad competition—the difference between competing at the broader industry level and competing more narrowly in a specific segment of the market. Competition at the highest levels—nationally and internationally—is largely carried out by industry leaders like Google, EBSCO, and the major book publishers. Libraries normally work within their own segments of the library market, whether it is a college campus, a city, or a school district. It is important, however, to define the specific markets you wish to serve as precisely as possible. Increased hours of operation for an academic library may be of greatest value to students escaping the dorms to study, for example, while access to highly specialized journals may be essential to only a few faculty members. It is important to channel the library's resources to those segments that will derive the greatest benefit. For more information, see page 113, the section on market segments.

For many librarians and library administrators, coping with an endless series of interlopers and squabbling over scraps of funding is an unwelcome, unaccustomed state of affairs. Nevertheless, for better or worse, all signs point to a future in which libraries will increasingly compete for the time and loyalty of library patrons. By approaching this challenge as a series of learnable skills and manageable tasks, and using the many strengths and talents librarians have at their disposal, there is little doubt that libraries can survive and thrive.

Facing Disruption

Related to the theme of competition is the concept of disruption. It is not unusual for practitioners in any field, even libraries, to face competitors who perform job tasks in much the same way as they do, competing on the same playing field under more or less the same rules. Occasionally, however, entire industries are upended and completely transformed by disruptive change. This might be the result of new technologies, new organizational structures, or new methodologies. When this happens, competition and threats may crash into an organization from wildly unpredictable sources and directions. Such upheaval can be disorienting, ripping away points of reference and leaving what appears to be unfathomable chaos. In recent decades, the most profound disruptions seem to arise from technology, including such innovations as personal computers, the Internet, and mobile smart devices. There are few jobs, or even individual tasks, that have not been impacted by the technological revolution of the last few decades. Disruptive innovation has reconfigured the world so often and so deeply that we risk becoming weary of it to the point of surrender. Many industries (libraries and education among them) have been hit by so many changes on such a regular basis that the practitioners seem almost punch-drunk, starting at imaginary trends and striking out at perceived threats. As with almost any other challenge, however, disruptive change can be managed—and even converted to an opportunity—given a working knowledge of the process and an appropriate plan of action.

Clayton Christensen is one of the leading authorities on disruption and disruptive innovation. In simplest terms, Christensen (1997) describes disruptive innovation as a situation in which a new entrant to the market starts off by competing at the bottom end, providing basic services or products in a more convenient way, and at a lower price, than the existing market leader. The market leader responds by focusing more on the upper end of the market, producing high-end products and services aimed at the most lucrative clients. Over time, the innovator gradually improves its services, taking more and more of the market, until the innovator drives the leader out of the market. Figure 7.3 illustrates the process.

Here a market leader (the incumbent) provides the services clients need. The incumbent continues to improve these services, often overshooting the needs of the clients and underserving those who need only basic services. Over time, an innovator shows up, offering services that better suit client needs, especially those at the lower end of the market. Eventually the innovator improves services at the upper end of the market as well, and comes to dominate the entire market. The model assumes that the innovator becomes the market leader and may, in turn, eventually succumb to overshooting the market and becoming vulnerable to future innovators.

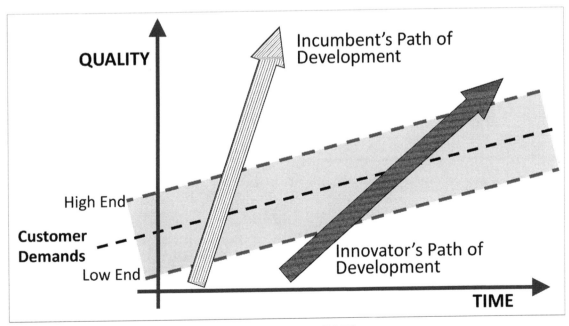

Figure 7.3.   Christensen's model of disruptive innovation (1997)

In a sense, this is what libraries experienced at the hands of disruptive innovators like Google and Wikipedia. To begin with, library books and journals offered more information, of a better quality, than Internet sources. The high quality of the library's resources was not valued by low-end users, however, who loved the convenience and free access of online services, and the quality of these low-end services was adequate for their needs. Internet services like Google and Wikipedia have, over time, used the power of the Internet to provide a better quality of materials in a more convenient way. Currently libraries still provide quality resources that are not available online but, in general, the distinction in quality is appreciated only by those carrying out research at the highest levels. Christensen holds that this is a pattern observed frequently in industry disruption: the complacent incumbent organization becomes vulnerable by focusing too heavily on high-end users, while the innovator provides inexpensive, easily accessible services at the low end. The innovator then uses the profits of low-cost domination to continue improving quality. By this logic, it might seem that libraries are doomed to extinction by the unstoppable juggernaut of low-cost Internet resources.

Not everyone agrees, however, that this pattern is as pervasive as Christensen and his supporters suggest. Writing for the *New Yorker*, Lepore (2014) observed that theories of innovative disruption have become so pervasive that virtually every established organization is now perceived to be lumbering prey that will inevitably fall to hungry, agile innovators. Lepore dismisses this dark, paranoid image, noting that Christensen's hand-picked anecdotes don't necessarily portray either the present or the future accurately. Disruptive events are, by their nature, unexpected and unprecedented—you can no more predict disruption using Christensen's models than you can predict the weather a year from now based solely on the weather this afternoon. In the real world, innovation arises in many ways—Apple's disruption of the market for mobile devices, for example, occurred when Apple had already been a technology leader for many years. King and Baatartogtokh (2015) asked industry experts to review 77 of the examples of innovative disruption identified by Christensen, and they found that fewer than 10 percent legitimately met all of Christensen's own criteria for innovative disruption. These researchers found many factors contributing to disruptive innovation, including changes in business conditions, shifts in the economy, and the emergence of new leaders. They concluded that innovative disruption theories can be useful for understanding the process of innovation, but in terms of predicting future disruptions, theories are no replacement for using critical thinking and careful analysis to make the hard decisions.

Fostering Healthy Innovation

If the grand theories of innovation are of limited value in predicting the future, it may seem that innovation is just a constant, unknowable threat—a meteor crashing without warning through the bedroom roof. Lewis (2006) notes that markets can't be analyzed if they don't yet exist, and experts who try to do so will be wrong. This does not mean, however, that your library's reference services must wait to be victimized by roving packs of innovators. Using rational methodologies and a bit of good judgment, you can manage innovation in your own library. What follows are a few basic strategies and tips for encouraging innovative thinking and activity throughout your library operations.

- *Have a motivating mission.* Nothing motivates people to come up with new ideas, and work hard to implement them, than passionate commitment to an ideal. If you can inspire your staff and colleagues to put themselves behind a challenge larger than themselves, their enthusiasm and determination can accomplish incredible things.

- *Know your market.* A theme that repeats itself throughout this book is the importance of understanding the needs of your clientele, whether they are business executives, faculty, students, seniors, children, or even other librarians. Everyone has problems to solve, and nothing creates more loyalty among library patrons than knowing that their library can provide cost-effective, enjoyable solutions. Be aware that this will require more than a simple demographic profile. You need to understand the problems your patrons face, and come up with new and effective methods of helping solve those problems. There is no shortcut—the only way to do this is by spending considerable time with your patrons, experiencing firsthand the obstacles they face. In this way you will neither overshoot nor undershoot the needs of your clientele.

- *Shake up existing relationships.* Change the assignments of staff, and change the membership of teams. New faces and different responsibilities will help to encourage fresh ways of looking at problems. Have people who don't normally work together try partnering on new projects. If you are not in a position to assign partners, make it a personal goal to seek out new partners and teams to face challenges. Leadership does not always come from the top—often it only takes one person to be a catalyst for others.

- *Be brave enough to play.* Many of the greatest innovations in history are accidents, or come about at unexpected moments. Take time to loosen up and try things—even things that may seem frivolous. This is why cutting-edge technology firms are renowned for providing their employees with toys and games, and encouraging off-topic behavior that might not be tolerated in a more conservative environment. Play is the way humans learn; it is the key to discovery. Give the gifts of time and the freedom to play around.

- *Be brave enough to fail.* A corollary of the need to play and experiment is the need to accept failure as a vital, welcome part of the process. While scientists love nothing more than a successful experiment, every successful scientist understands that you learn far more from a failed experiment than a successful one. Librarians should approach their own experimentation no differently. Try new solutions . . . lots of them! Keep your experiments small and manageable, perhaps in the form of pilot projects. Don't invest so much in any one experiment that the fear of failure creeps back in. If your pilot project does fail, do not use failure as an excuse to give up. Instead, take a moment to consider what went wrong and what could be done to fix it. Then move quickly to try again.

- *Let everyone play.* In many organizations, creative activity is the province of an elite group of individuals, often hand-picked as future leaders. It is vital to expand the right to play to the broadest group possible. The support of senior staff and administration is an important element of any innovative project, but make the effort to include all of your staff, interns, student assistants, patrons, and anyone else who has an interest. Try throwing out an invitation on the library website, or using flyers throughout the building and across your community. Getting input from a broader range of participants also has the added benefit of helping to achieve buy-in from a broader range of stakeholders. Finally, make sure that everyone who has contributed to the project in any way receives fitting credit for their work.

- *Foster innovation in real terms.* Encourage your staff to be creative and try new approaches by allocating time and resources to innovation. Make sure the staff have the time to think about new approaches, and at least minimal funds to pursue their ideas. Ensure that staff members who develop successful projects are rewarded appropriately. Even if you cannot provide lucrative financial rewards, be lavish in praise and recognition of new and helpful ideas. It is, in fact, wise to go one step further and support *all* creative thinking and activity, regardless of outcome. Encourage creative experimentation as a behavior, in other words, because rewarding only the most successful projects simply leads you back to a fear of failure. When your staff understands that creativity is important to the organization, then creativity will become more important to them.

⊚ Future Technology

It should be obvious that technology is central to both the current practice and future direction of library reference services. As discussed repeatedly throughout this book, technology often arrives as an unexpected disruption, overturning the way libraries operate and transforming the lives of librarians and their patrons. While it is not possible to predict technological innovations with anything approaching accuracy, it is always fascinating to discuss what might come to pass. Will drone "librarians" buzz books directly to our homes? Will articles be flashed directly to chips implanted in our brains? For those inclined to scoff at such ideas, be aware that Flirtey, an Australian startup, has proposed using its drone technology to partner with book-rental service Zookal to deliver books directly to clients. In the United States, researchers at the Massachusetts Institute of Technology and Microsoft have developed temporary tattoos that can interact with smart phones and computers, while researchers at the University of Southern California are experimenting with implanting computer chips in those suffering from brain disorders like Alzheimer's disease and epilepsy to enhance mental functioning. While it is true that these projects are all at an embryonic stage, at least some of today's craziest outsiders will end up as tomorrow's respected visionaries.

It is not necessary, however, to travel far into the realm of speculative science to find technological innovations that will affect the daily operation of libraries. The number of emerging and future technologies with the potential to transform libraries is nearly infinite, but the items listed here are likely to be game changers for library reference services in the near future:

- *Virtual reference.* While virtual reference has been available for some years in the form of instant messaging and chat, there are always new products and approaches to consider. It is an unfortunate but perennial truth that libraries are often relatively slow to pick up on improvements and innovations that have been available to the public in other contexts, often for many months or years. Kik, for example, is an instant-messaging app that is particularly popular among millennials, largely due to the inclusion of a useful Internet browser within the app that makes it easier to share websites and content. In recent years, some library journal articles have suggested that the use of chat systems for reference has never really gained popularity among users or librarians, but most technology experts agree that the popularity of chat among young users indicates that it will eventually replace email as the primary means of text communication. Now is a good time to review the many chat innovations available on the market in preparation for the inevitable demands that will arise for libraries in the coming years.

- *Open access and repositories.* Among the most treasured ideals of librarians is free, open access to articles, books, dissertations, and other research materials. Open access could free libraries from paying exorbitant fees to publishers for content that is often created and edited for free by academics. It is important to point out that the open access movement is important to all libraries, not just those that serve academics. All libraries retrieve articles on topics related to health, business, science, and every other academic discipline. One pressing challenge for librarians is identifying and locating these articles when they are posted. Many open access materials are placed in library repositories, and searching through every repository in the nation, or the world, can be a daunting task. One good source is OpenDOAR (opendoar.org), a directory of academic open access repositories searchable by institution and content. Graduate theses and dissertations are also provided through open access, but can be similarly difficult to find. In addition to commercial aggregators providing access to graduate publications, OATD.org offers searchable access to over 1100 colleges, universities, and research institutions, indexing 3,280,873 theses and dissertations as of this writing. Google Scholar also provides many open access materials, with the added benefit of a number of useful tutorials to help users set up and get the most out of Google products.

- *The Deep Web.* Reference librarians will be increasingly challenged in the years to come by materials buried beyond the bounds of Google and Bing on the Internet. This whole realm is sometimes referred to as the Deep Web, which must be distinguished from the Dark Web. The term Dark Web carries a connotation of illegality, immorality, and toxicity; most librarians will never find a need for the Dark Web. The Deep Web, on the other hand, simply refers to those parts of the Internet that may be hidden or restricted for other reasons. Library databases through such vendors as EBSCO and ProQuest are part of the Deep Web, as are organizational intranets closed to all but their authorized users. Some of the open access repositories discussed above may be hidden from common search engines, making them a part of the Deep Web as well. As web resources become more varied, and the means of accessing them become more complex, librarians will be called on to become experts in finding the unfindable, and knowing the unknowable, even in corners of the web far outside the library.

- *Radio Frequency Identification (RFID) tags.* RFID tags contain a very small computer chip and a radio antenna, and can replace both barcode readers and security tags for books and other library materials. They are used to increase the efficiency and accuracy of checkout, security, and inventory management. They are helpful for reference services in that they can be used to track the location of specific materials, even if those materials are misplaced in any corner of the library. RFID is expensive, and early versions suffered some minor problems, but they are likely to become a common tool for libraries in the future.

The technological innovations listed above could become important parts of librarianship in the coming years, or they may fade away without a trace. Thousands of other innovations may take their place at any moment, and there is, unfortunately, no crystal ball to tell us which will survive. The best way to keep up with technology in libraries, as is the case in so many areas of life, is to remain open to possibilities—play with new products and applications whenever you can, and incorporate those innovations that turn out to be both useful and cost-effective. Those that don't contribute efficiently to your efforts should be discarded, however trendy they may be. Take time to review options carefully; remember that there are few rewards for early adoption of technologies, but many potential penalties for taking on an unproven prototype.

⊚ Future Services

Similar to controversies concerning the future of library technology, there is no shortage of debate about the future of library reference services. What should become of the old reference desk? Make it into a planter or a bench, as we did with the beautiful old card catalog? What of the other library services? Can librarians actually answer questions that Google can't? There are thousands of competing predications about the future of reference services, all based on conflicting evidence, collectively resulting in an almost complete lack of consensus on any given issue. This lack of agreement, while stress-inducing, does carry with it a degree of freedom and opportunity for those open to new perspectives. It becomes more difficult with each passing year for any librarian to say, "That's just the way we've always done things here, and we're not changing now." Librarians will face many serious obstacles in the coming years, and success will require flexibility, creativity, and an ongoing willingness to seek new and better solutions for every challenge.

While it may not be possible to provide accurate predictions about the future of reference services, it is relatively easy to identify some intriguing possibilities. Below are just a few of the changes reference services might see in the coming years:

- *The old reference desk.* As previously mentioned, the reference desk has already been eliminated or transformed in many libraries. Some libraries have moved to one-point service at a main desk, where general staff handle simple questions but hand off complex questions to reference librarians. Others have suggested that library assistance should be carried out exclusively online via chat, text, and social media. There is also experimentation with roving reference staff moving throughout the library, using mobile devices to help patrons with research and reference, and to locate books and other physical items. In general terms, the reference desk is a recognizable and possibly comforting destination for some, but it is not essential to providing reference services.
- *We have an app for that.* In recent years it seems that every function in life has acquired its own collection of mobile apps. We use them for exercising, shopping, praying, eating, and even sleeping. It should come as no surprise, therefore, that we have begun to see the release of many library-related apps that can be loaded on smartphones and other mobile devices. A recent study by the Pew Research Center (Zickuhr, Rainie, and Purcell, 2013: 3) reports that 35 percent of Americans ages 16 and older would "very likely" use app-based access to library materials and programs, while another 28 percent say they would be "somewhat likely" to do so. An example of app-based access to library materials is BrowZine, which allows library users to find and read journals. It works as an online reader, similar to Amazon's Kindle, and allows easy browsing of specific issues of journals and periodicals. BrowZine is available for Apple iOS, Android, and Kindle tablets. Many

library-related apps are currently in release, or close to it, and the growth in this area should be strong in the future.

- *Behavior-based recommendations for library materials.* Along the same lines as app-based access to library materials are what many call "Amazon-style" customized book/audio/video recommendation schemes. These services would provide recommendations to library patrons based on their previous activity at the library. If you read a book about New York City, for example, the service might recommend other books about New York City, or guide you to materials used by other patrons who have previously read books about New York. According to the Pew Research Center (Zickuhr, Rainie, and Purcell, 2013: 3), 29 percent of Americans ages 16 and older would "very likely" use that service, while another 35 percent say they would be "somewhat likely" to do so.
- *Flexible spaces.* Given the popular focus on technology and technological innovation, it is important to note that many of the physical trappings of reference services will remain useful for many years to come. Even the most futuristically minded library theorists recognize that the library as a physical space remains extremely important. There is increasing recognition that the library is not simply a storage warehouse for old books and magazines—libraries are being reimagined as centers of collaboration and creativity, where people come together to develop new ideas and projects. Knowledge is increasingly viewed as a cooperative evolutionary process, not as a collection of static library materials. Libraries of the future can act as the perfect incubator for this new approach to knowledge creation. In addition to mobile technologies, many libraries are experimenting with moveable chairs, furniture, and even moveable walls—allowing library spaces to conform to patron needs, not the other way around.
- *Flexible services.* Alternate approaches to the reference desk are discussed above, but there are many opportunities open to reference librarians who look beyond traditional definitions of librarianship. Reference librarians have embedded themselves in political and social organizations, becoming invaluable as experts in specialized reference and research. Librarians are using library resources and skills to help both existing businesses and start-ups, researching demographics, business regulations, and thousands of other details to contribute both to the success of specific businesses, and to the overall fiscal well-being of their communities.

There were times in the last few decades when, to be charitable, the future of libraries seemed in doubt. Library detractors were quick to point out that libraries were known primarily as repositories of paper products—books and magazines and perhaps some old vinyl recordings—and if paper is obsolete, then the library must, by extension, be obsolete as well. In more recent years, however, libraries have been reborn as curators of paper collections that still need tending, as shepherds of information technology with its ever-increasing variety and unruliness, and even as matchmakers for the many creative minds required to achieve success in a complicated modern world.

◎ Key Points

Reference services are positioned now exactly as they have always been, at the frontlines of the library, helping patrons make sense of the endless sea of resources available to them.

This need will always remain in one form or another, and librarians must always be first responders.

- Library reference services in the future must become whatever they need to become to continue to provide their patrons—especially the most vulnerable among them—with the support and space they need to achieve their goals.
- Libraries must learn to compete against other resources and agencies to secure a place in the future, gathering and presenting effective evidence of the value they provide to those that fund and support them.
- Reference services staff must vigilantly look for disruptive innovations that will change their environment, and learn to encourage the messy, chaotic process of creative innovation in their own organizations.
- Innovative technology, in particular, will continue to drive changes in reference services and in all areas of library operations.
- While technology will continue to remain a powerful force in the future, it is ultimately the effectiveness and responsiveness of library services that will dictate the success of libraries in the future.

References

Argyres, Nicholas, and Anita M. McGahan. 2002. "An Interview with Michael Porter." *Academy of Management Executive* 16, no. 2: 43–52.

Christensen, Clayton M. 1997. *The Innovator's Dilemma: When New Technologies Cause Great Firms to Fail.* Boston: Harvard Business School Press.

Ewing, Keith, and Robert Hauptman. 1995. "Is Traditional Reference Service Obsolete?" *Journal of Academic Librarianship* 21, no. 1: 3–6.

Gorman, Michael. 2012. "The Prince's Dream: A Future for Academic Libraries." *New Review of Academic Librarianship* 18, no. 2: 114–26.

Kenney, Brian. 2015. "For Future Reference." *Publishers Weekly* 262, no. 37: 20–21.

King, Andrew A., and Baljir Baatartogtokh. 2015. "How Useful Is the Theory of Disruptive Innovation?" *MIT Sloan Management Review* 57, no. 1: 77–90.

Koerber, Jennifer. 2016. "MIT's Future of the Library: Encouraging Social Knowledge-Building." *Library Journal,* March 3. http://lj.libraryjournal.com/2016/03/future-of-libraries/mits-future-of-the-library-encouraging-social-knowledge-building/.

Lankes, R. David. 2012. "Libraries Are Obsolete." *OLA Quarterly* 18, no. 2: 12–17.

Lepore, Jill. 2014. "The Disruption Machine: What the Gospel of Innovation Gets Wrong." *New Yorker* 90, no. 17: 30–31.

Lewis, David W. 1995. "Traditional Reference Is Dead, Now Let's Move on to Important Questions." *Journal of Academic Librarianship* 21, no. 1: 10–12.

———. 2006. "Disruptive Innovation and Academic Libraries." Presentation, Living the Future 6 Conference, Tucson, AZ, April 6. http://arizona.openrepository.com/arizona/handle/10150/222274.

Porter, Michael E. 1980. *Competitive Strategy: Techniques for Analyzing Industries and Competitors.* New York: Free Press.

Zickuhr, Kathryn, Lee Rainie, and Kristen Purcell. 2013. *Library Services in the Digital World* (Report). Washington, DC: Pew Research Center. http://libraries.pewinternet.org/2013/01/22/library-services/.

Index

administration of reference services: documenting performance and achievements, xiv; leadership vs. management, 90; middle management, 87–88; roles of reference supervisors, 88–90. *See also* assessment of reference services; budgets

American Library Association (ALA), 5–6, 12, 16, 24

assessment of reference services: assessment cycle, *106*; benefits, 100; data analysis, 105–6; data collection tools, 103–5; data types, 101–2; developing an assessment plan, 100–101; use of data, 105–6

Association of Research Libraries (ARL), 2

budgets: cost control, 99; library budgets, 94, *95*; reference services budget, 98–99, *98*; staffing budget, 65

CD-ROM indexes, 13, 32

Chicago library budget cuts in 1930s, 97

Christensen, Clayton, 139–40

clientele. *See* patrons

collaboration for reference services, 123–28; definition, 123–24; developing collaborations, 125–26; effects on staff, 124–25; libraries as partners, 124; sample memorandum of understanding, *127*; types of collaborations, 126–28

Collins, Jim, 68

communication. *See* marketing for reference services; staff management

competition: 133–38; Porter's competitive forces, 133–36, *134*; Porter's competitive strategies, 137–38, *137*

content management systems, 38–39

data collection, 102; job analysis, 70–72; market research, 114–18, *116*, *118*; methods of data collection, 103–5. *See also* assessment of reference services

Desk Set (film), 11–12

Discovery systems, 35–37

disruption: Christensen's model of disruptive innovation, *139*; disruption for reference services, 139–40; innovators and incumbents, 139; prediction of future disruption, 140

documentation. *See* data collection

emotional intelligence quotient (EQ), 48–52

future of reference services: future services, 144–45; future technology, 142–44. *See also* competition; disruption

Google and reference services, viii, 29–30, 32–33, 35–36, 57, 58, 104, 120, 131, 135, 138, 140, 143–44

HathiTrust, 35

hiring. *See* selection, personnel

hours of operation, 65

human resources. *See* staff management

innovation in reference services, 140–42

Internet, 3, 15–16, 28–30, 32

Jagd, Soren, 90

Katz, William A., 12–14, 24

About the Authors

John Gottfried is a faculty librarian and associate professor at Western Kentucky University. He is the reference services coordinator and business librarian for WKU Libraries. He completed his master of library science degree at Indiana University, Indianapolis, and his master of business administration and master's degree in organizational management at the University of Colorado at Denver. He has authored book chapters on time management for librarians and on the use of free electronic resources to help library patrons. He has also published articles in a number of academic journals, including the *Journal of Academic Librarianship*, *Reference and User Services Quarterly*, *Reference Librarian*, and *Business and Finance Librarianship*.

Katherine Pennavaria is a faculty librarian and professor at Western Kentucky University. She earned a bachelor's degree in English from DePauw University, a master's degree in English from the University of Missouri–Kansas City, and a master of library science degree from Indiana University–Bloomington. After 13 years as the coordinator of the WKU regional campus library in Glasgow, Kentucky, she became the coordinator of the Visual and Performing Arts Library on the main campus in Bowling Green. She is author of *Genealogy: A Practical Guide for Librarians* (Rowman & Littlefield, 2015), and writes a regular column on genealogy for *Kentucky Libraries*.